LOAN

PAPER BASICS:

Forestry, Manufacture, Selection, Purchasing, Mathematics and Metrics, Recycling

PAPER BASICS:

Forestry, Manufacture, Selection, Purchasing, Mathematics and Metrics, Recycling

David Saltman

VNR **VAN NOSTRAND REINHOLD COMPANY**
NEW YORK   CINCINNATI   ATLANTA   DALLAS   SAN FRANCISCO
LONDON   TORONTO   MELBOURNE

Printed on Whitestone Offset, Basis 60#, supplied by Nucross Papers, the first quality division of Cross Siclare/New York, Inc.

Van Nostrand Reinhold Company Regional Offices:
New York Cincinnati Atlanta Dallas San Francisco

Van Nostrand Reinhold Company International Offices:
London Toronto Melbourne

Library of Congress Catalog Card Number: 78-1476
ISBN : 0-442-25121-1
        0-442-25124-6 pbk.

Manufactured in the United States of America

Published by Van Nostrand Reinhold Company
135 West 50th Street, New York, N. Y. 10020

Published simultaneously in Canada by Van Nostrand Reinhold Ltd.

15 14 13 12 11 10 9 8 7 6 5 4 3 2 1

Library of Congress Cataloging in Publication Data

Saltman, David.
    Paper basics.

    Includes index.
    1. Paper. I. Title.
TS1105.S23   676.2 78-1476
ISBN 0-442-25121-1
ISBN 0-442-25124-6 pbk.

TO
Gilbert and Elliot
Barbara, Michelle and Kenneth
and Elaine

ACKNOWLEDGMENTS

I wish to acknowledge, with thanks, the assistance of the following organizations:

Allied Paper Company
American Forest Institute
American Paper Institute
Beloit Corporation
Bergstrom Paper Company
Black Clawson Company
Boise Cascade Corp.
Brown Company
Canadian Pulp and Paper Association
Case Paper Company
Champion International Corporation
Cross Siclare/New York
Environmental Protection Agency
Finch, Pruyn & Company
Hammermill Paper Company
Harris Economy Group of American
  Hoist
Institute of Paper Chemistry
International Paper Company
Jagenberg (U.S.A.)
Kamyr Incorporated
Major Paper Converters
Mead Corporation
Milton Paper Company
National Association of Recycling
  Industries

Nekoosa Papers, Inc.
Northwest Paper Division, Potlatch
  Corporation
Paper Industry Information Office,
  State of Maine
Potlatch Corporation
Rocky Mountain Forest and Range
  Experiment Station
St. Regis Paper Company
Scott Paper Company
Simpson Lee Paper Company
Strathmore Paper Company
Technical Association of the Pulp and
  Paper Industry
U.S. Department of Agriculture
    Forest Products Laboratory
    U.S. Forest Service
Warren, S. D. Company
Western Wood Products Association
Westvaco Corporation
Wisconsin Paper Council
Wantagh Public Library and the
  Nassau Library System

PREFACE

Understanding paper, from beginning to end, is what this book is about.

At the beginning we have discussed the forest, how we harvest it, how much of it we have, and why it is necessary to understand the problems associated with it. Smokey the Bear was wrong because fire is good for the forest when the fire can be controlled. Mature trees must be harvested to make room for new growth; otherwise Nature will harvest the trees in its own way—by wildfire, blowdown and insect infestation.

Trees are a renewable resource and we must use them wisely; by reseeding, replanting superior trees, and exercising good forest management after cutting.

Next we get into the basic understanding of the technology of papermaking, separating the fiber from the wood and weaving it into paper for printing. Most paper buyers and users take this fact for granted, so we spend some time discussing how to buy paper and how to make the best use of it. This is important, because the art of substitution of one grade for another, or the intelligent knowledge of when to use the various grades, will serve the dual purpose of obtaining the right paper for the right job or making another choice when the budget is tight or the grade is not available.

Paper Metrics will introduce you to the new way of designating paper, since we are now in the transition stage. Further, the table showing each grade and weight will give at a glance a quick reference to the possible art of substitution. A good example is the comparison of 20 lb bond to 50 lb offset—75 vs. 74 grams per square meter, respectively—equal in weight for practical purposes and interchangeable in many cases.

Job lot paper is as important to the paper industry as used cars are to automobile manufacturers, yet the subject has been neglected. We are bringing information to our readers without specific recommendation. There are situations where paper buyers have to become paper sellers when circumstances change, to give but one example.

Finally, conservation of our natural resources, concern for the environment, and recycling of paper after it has served its initial purpose are problems which will be with us well beyond the end of the century. In addition, all of these problems have a strong bearing on paper costs.

That is why this book has been written. I hope you find it both enjoyable and educational.

DAVID SALTMAN

CONTENTS

1
THE FOREST

Without the trees in the forest, paper as we know it today would not exist.

Paper is indispensable to contemporary life. The recording of words, illustrations, and photographs in books, periodicals, and newspapers is a measurement of a nation's literacy and living standards. Trees and technology have made such recording possible.

Fortunately, trees are a renewable resource. They can be harvested, and new trees will grow again in a period of years. Yet the simplicity of that statement is devastating, a half truth which hides the full story of a bounteous natural resource.

*   *   *   *

A tree, like a human being, is a living organism. It has a life span that varies with and within its species. Its life depends variously on its environment, climate, temperature, and circumstance. At some point in its life span it will reach the peak of its maturity, and its growth will cease; at that point its usefulness in the life cycle will end. As a growing organism a tree consumes carbon dioxide and releases oxygen. During growth it has many functions in the life cycle: acting as a haven for wildlife, regulating the flow of water, offering recreation to mankind, and much more.

Almost everyone has taken for granted the idea that trees are there when we need them—everyone, that is, except the people in the forest products industry. They are concerned about the future of the forest and have planted more than *three billion trees* to prove it. Furthermore, that figure will double and triple in the years to come.

Life Cycle of a Tree

Let us go back a few centuries in time, a very short period in forest history. On the North American continent, the population was a minute fraction of what it is today. When a tree reached its full growth, or maturity, it died. It could no longer absorb the nutrition of the soil or the energy of the sun. It could not consume carbon dioxide and convert it to cellulose while releasing oxygen.

The tree weakened. Insects found the dead tree a haven and gnawed away at its interior. The protective bark could no longer do its job. Then a strong wind would come along, and if the insects had had sufficient time to destroy their victim, the tree would fall to the ground. The fallen tree was now an additional liability—whatever lay in its path could not grow; wildlife shunned such an area as undesirable. Still, it took years for full tree rot to set in because nature is not in any hurry. Multiply this many times in an overmature area and you have a jungle of dead trees, fallen tree limbs, an overabundance of insects. Where does it end?

Nature does not stand still even though it moves slowly in its own way. The debris that litters the ground along with the fallen trees is a natural tinderbox. At some time lightning will strike, and a forest fire will result. Such a fire is uncontrollable because there is no way to stop it. It is commonly called wildfire.

Now, with the fire, the dead tree problem has been solved. The area has been cleared. Seeds that have lain dormant for years will spring to life, and a new cycle will begin. The debris that fell to the ground, the leaves, pine needles and branches, has been decomposing, refertilizing the soil. The fire has speeded up the process. The stage has been set for new life to begin.

Paper Consumption

Nature is wasteful. Man cannot afford this luxury. The consumption of paper is at an all-time high of 650 lb per capita per year and will reach 1,000 lb per capita in the next generation. Trees are also needed for lumber to build homes, furniture, plywood, industrial uses, and thousands of other necessities.

Forest products comprise approximately one-fifth of all industrial raw materials used in the United States today. Trees are unique because they are a renewable resource. Other raw materials are limited in quantity and are nonrenewable.

Our problem, therefore, is to ensure that our source of forest products is always available when needed. If we cut down trees faster than we grow them, we will be depleting a natural resource. So let us go back just a bit further and determine where the trees are, how much of this resource is available, just what the picture is. Then we can better understand the problem and its logical solutions.

Forest Statistics

In the United States, about one-third of the land is forest. Of this area, the eastern half accounts for more than 60% of the forest land.

In Canada, the forest totals about 1,700,000 square miles, or more than half of the land area. This large area is mostly uninhabited in the northern sector, but nevertheless accounts for one-tenth of the world's productive forests.

Regarding *commercial* timber holdings in the United States, refer to Figure 1-1. Of the 500 million acres available, note that the lion's

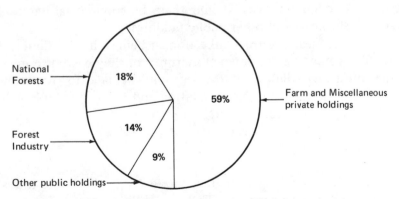

Figure 1-1. U.S. commercial holdings of timber total 500,000,000 acres, with ownership and percentages indicated.

share of 59% belongs to farms and miscellaneous private ownership. The national forests come second with only 18%, while the forest products industry represents but 14%.

Now study Figure 1-2. The most striking statistic here is that the forest products industry has accounted for 28% of the commercial timber harvested, while holding only 14% of the land area. All other areas harvested less.

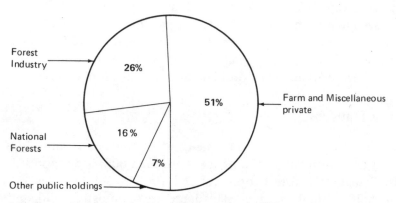

Figure 1-2. Timber harvesting in 1970 totaled 12,200,000 cubic feet. Note percentage of harvest compared with ownership above.

Does this mean that the forest industry, with the profit motive in mind, has been depleting its percentage of holdings at a faster rate? Also, for that matter, why should there be commercial harvests in the national forests and other public holdings?

As we stated earlier, trees, like human beings, have a limited life span. Trees must be cut down at maturity or they become a menace to the forest and wildlife. With a constant demand for forest products that increases with the population and living standards, where will the raw material come from?

Silviculture

This problem has long been recognized by both private industry and federal and state agencies. The answer lies in proper forest management, the science of silviculture. (Silviculture is defined as *a*

phase of forestry that deals with the establishment, development, re-
production, and care of forest trees.)

In line with this definition, it is the practice of the forest industry
to plan many years ahead, to ensure that there will be enough raw
material to meet the ever growing demand. This is done mainly, at
present, by planting superior trees to replace the ones that have been
harvested. A superior tree is a carefully selected strain that is first
grown in a nursery. This is done both by the U.S. Forest Service and
the forest products industry. One such tree is shown in Figure 1-3.

Figure 1-3. Tree grown as a result of silviculture method by Brunswick Pulp & Paper Company, Brunswick, Georgia. Brunswick is owned jointly by Scott Paper Company and the
Mead Corporation. (*Courtesy Scott Paper Company*)

Timber Use

It is interesting to note the use of timber by major categories, as shown in Figure 1-4. Saw timber ranks highest, with pulpwood running second. Also note that softwood is used to a much greater extent than hardwood in every category except fuelwood. Softwood also grows faster, with a much shorter maturity time.

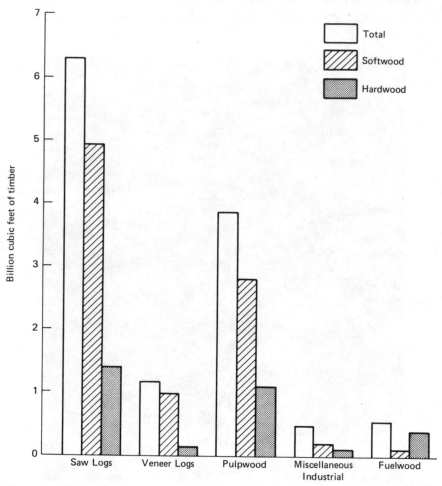

Figure 1-4. Timber harvest in 1970 by category of use. Note that pulpwood in both softwood and hardwood combined is just under 32% of the timber harvest. Also note the predominant use of softwood over hardwood in all but the fuelwood category.

Hardwoods

Perhaps you are puzzled by the terms *soft* and *hard* wood. Hardwoods can be easily identified in the warmer season (spring and summer) as broadleaf types. Their leaves are shed in the fall, the trees are bare in the winter, and a new growth emerges in the spring. Some examples of hardwood trees are maple, oak, and birch.

Softwoods

Softwoods, on the other hand, are evergreens, with needles instead of leaves. Examples are pine, spruce, hemlock, and fir. The seeds from these trees are found in cones; hence they are often referred to as conifers.

Despite the fact that trees are a renewable resource, there will always be the problem of whether the supply can keep pace with the demand. In this respect we might look at some charts in order to get a better perspective. In Figure 1-5 we have shown a projection of the anticipated demand, as it was in 1970 and what we anticipate the demand will be at the end of the century. Note again that the total need is expected to double.

Harvesting in Public Lands

There are great misconceptions, especially among serious-minded conservationists, that commercial greed is overtaking and destroying our forests. These people decry the fact that not only is the forest products industry cutting down trees for industrial use, but also the government is allowing some portion of national forest areas to be commercially harvested. Of course there may well be some abuses of improper harvesting, but one must be practical about the advantages of harvesting in public lands. Some of these advantages are:

1. Overmature areas are cleared to make room for new growth.
2. The government derives revenue from the wood cut and removed by private industry.
3. Mature trees, if not removed, will be a breeding ground for insects and subject to destruction by windstorm and wildfire.

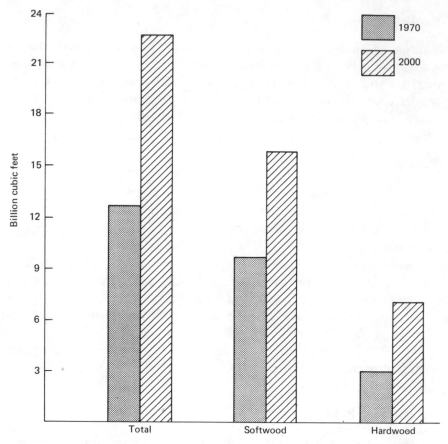

Figure 1-5. Projection of timber requirements for the United States from 1970 to the year 2000.

4. Mature trees absorb very little carbon dioxide and consume oxygen. They take up valuable space and shut out sunlight needed by the younger, growing trees.

Figure 1-6 reveals some interesting facts. Note that there were actual increases in available timber from 1952 to 1962 to 1970. While no later statistics are available at this writing, we can hopefully assume that this trend is continuing as it has in the past.

Canadian Forests

Returning to our neighbor to the north, we have a projection of timber harvesting ranging from about 4.2 billion cubic feet in 1970

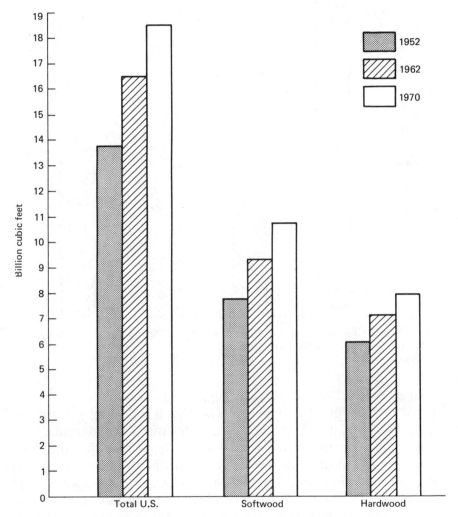

Figure 1-6. Chart showing net growth of softwood and hardwood and total of both between 1952 and 1970.

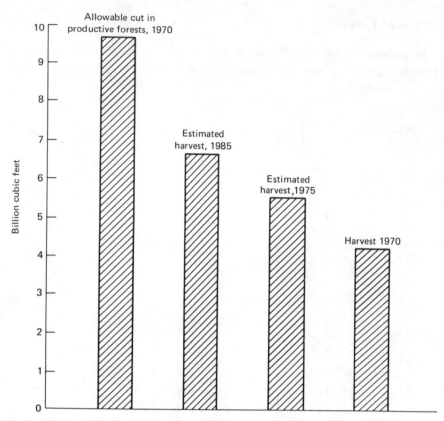

Figure 1-7. Projection of timber harvest in Canada from 1970 to 1985. It is estimated that the productive forest area increases each year.

to an estimate of harvest 15 years later that anticipates an increase of approximately 59% (see Figure 1-7). This is a healthy sign for the United States, since it imports pulp and newsprint from Canada.

Regarding ownership of Canadian forest land, note that the provinces own the most, with the federal crown government a poor second, as shown in Figure 1-8. Private holdings occupy a weak third place, with only about 7% of the total. In contrast, U.S. governmental holdings (federal, state, municipal, and so on) are about 27%, the U.S. forest products industry owns 14% (Figure 1-1), while our miscellaneous private ownership is the largest single category with 59%.

Alaskan Forests

To round out the picture, the state of Alaska shows over 100 million acres of forest land, but only one-fourth of it has growth potential, as shown in Figure 1-9. This land is considered negligible for statistical purposes for reasons of geography and economics. However, one never knows what the future may hold. If the price of raw timber accelerates as did the cost of petroleum, the picture may change. Furthermore, the process of *converting trees into*

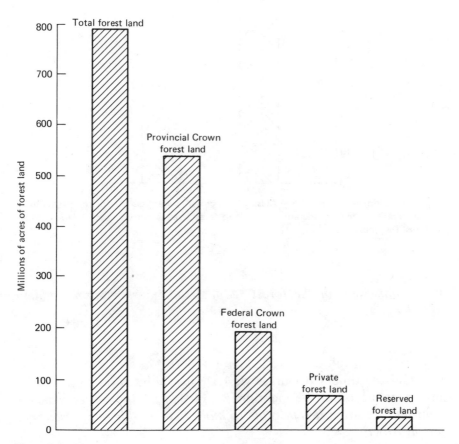

Figure 1-8. Forest land area in Canada and its ownership, 1970.

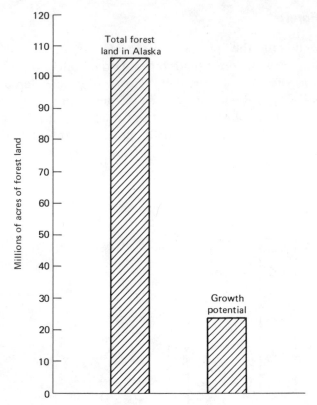

Figure 1-9. Estimated forest land in Alaska, with growth potential. because of geographical location and economic considerations, this land forest area is not included in U.S. productive forest statistics.

wood chips right in the forest reduces the transportation problem considerably.

Growth and Harvest

Besides the timber resources we have just pointed out, a few other important facts must be mentioned. First, *with intensified management and research, it is possible to more than double our present net annual growth.*

While the forest industries have led the way in timber harvests in proportion to land ownership, they only averaged 52 cubic feet per acre in 1970.   This is about 60% of the average attainable in fully stocked natural stands and about one-third of what it could be in intensively managed forests!

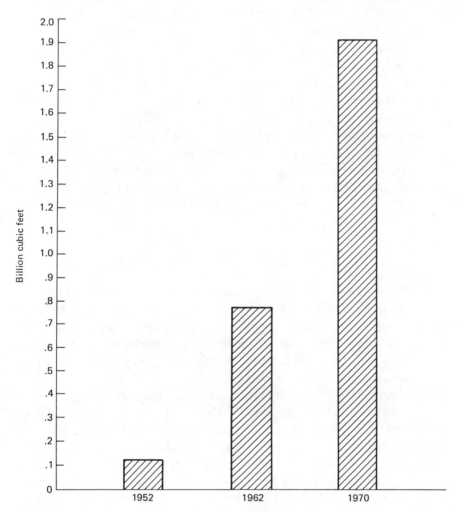

Figure 1-10. Wood residue from sawmills converted to wood chips and used as pulpwood. Note the tremendous expansion from 1952 to 1970.

Even worse, the acreage owned by farm and miscellaneous private ownerships averaged only 36 cubic feet per acre in net annual growth. This is extremely poor for a land area of 296 million acres. As we saw in Figure 1-1, this classification represents a huge 59% of the nation's woodlands.

The national forests and other public holdings are also far below their potential harvesting capabilities. Is it asking too much to have the respective governmental agencies, which derive revenue from allowable harvest, plow this income back into the ground in the form of sound management practice, thinning out crowded areas, and building roads to control forest growth? Strangely enough, this same sound management practice will, in turn, generate increased revenue to *more than pay for a sound silvicultural program*!

The problem of forest revenue and outlay is strictly one to be resolved by the legislative bodies in Washington!

Another asset in our wood use program is the recycling of our forest products where feasible. While this is a subject covered in a later chapter, we might mention some of the good news at this point.

Utilizing Waste Timber

In Figure 1-4 we showed the timber harvest in 1970 by category of use. Note the amount or percentage of wood used as saw logs and veneer logs. In saw timber, visualize a round circle, which might represent the cross section of a tree. From this circle, we cut squares or rectangles for use as saw lumber, the rest being waste. In veneer logs, we consider the cores to be waste.

In Figure 1-10, note the conversion of the commercial lumber waste described in the paragraph above. Instead of there being a solid waste product left for disposal, a great deal of the unusable wood waste is now converted to wood chips right at the source. These chips, in turn, are sold to the pulp and paper mills as pulpwood. This program has been so successful that the use of wood chips in 1970 was almost 18 times as great as in 1952. Although no official statistics are available as of this writing, it is our belief that the quantity of wood chips used is still growing, although probably not at such a rapid pace as shown in Figure 1-10.

Figure 1-11. Felling a big ponderosa pine. (*Courtesy Western Wood Products Assn.*)

Forest Mortality

The other side of the coin is not as heartening. The mortality factor of forests is that approximately one-fifth of the annual growth is lost owing to natural hazards—namely, fire, insects, and blowdown. Much of this mortality is in the national forests where too much of the area is both overmature and inaccessible. (Figure 1-11 shows the felling of a big ponderosa pine.)

The mortality rate of our timber can be lessened by building roads through the forests (see Figure 1-12). If more areas were accessible, forest fires and insects could be more easily controlled. Human recreation areas could be expanded. A sound silvicultural program would also enhance the population of wildlife because they would find the forests more inviting.

Multiple Use

This is what we mean by the multiple use concept—use of the forest for recreation, wildlife, watershed protection, livestock grazing, and a source for wood products. The forest products industries open their lands to human recreation as a matter of good public relations. National and state parks are meant to be recreation areas.

Figure 1-12. Truck with a load of logs going from the forest to the mill. (*Courtesy Western Wood Products Assn.*)

A small body of people would leave more and more of our forests as *wilderness* areas. This is fine for *much less than 1% of the population*. All the disadvantages of the overmature and unmanaged forest weigh heavily against this concept.

2

HARVEST AND NEW GROWTH

In Chapter 1 we emphasized the importance of the forest as a continuing source of wood supply. Harvesting methods are a vital part of the overall plan, since we do not harvest without due consideration of how we shall continue to grow trees where the old ones once stood.

To the layman, the common sense approach to harvesting would be to pick out a mature tree, cut it down, then haul it to the mill. The forester, on the other hand, would ask many questions, such as:

1. How far are these trees from an access road?
2. How can we get tree-removal equipment into the area?
3. Can the tree be felled easily, or will it be hampered by many other trees around it?
4. What damage will be done to the young, growing trees by the heavy duty, tractor-type equipment?
5. Is this the most economical and practical method of harvesting?

There are many more considerations, of course, which we shall point out as we progress. In the meantime, observe the photos in Figures 2-1, 2-2, and 2-3, which will give the reader some idea of the

Figure 2-1. A skidder at work. The blade on front can be used to rough out roads, but is mainly used for piling logs in yarding areas. (*Courtesy S. D. Warren Co.*)

type of equipment that is used in the logging operation. This picture is far from complete, since there are many methods of tree cutting and tree removal.

We shall now discuss harvesting methods, with the first to be considered *selective cutting*.

Selective Cutting

A forester goes through a given stand, selects trees for harvest and marks them accordingly. As the situation implies, this would occur in an area where the trees are of different ages, many of them still growing and not yet ready for harvesting. We refer to this type of area as an *uneven-age stand.*

The advantages of this method of harvest are obvious—only mature trees are cut, leaving the forest in a pleasing state for the public eye. Also, after the removal of older growth, younger trees have more room to grow, and more sunlight filters through the overhead tree cover.

Figure 2-2. This mechanical tree harvester does the work of many men in Scott's Northeast Operations. Almost in the blink of an eye, the harvester's piston-driven blade shoots up the tree, trimming away the limbs. A hydraulic sheet clips off the tree's top and then cuts the tree itself. (*Courtesy S. D. Warren Co.*)

Figure 2-3. TH-105 thinner-harvester. It can cut, delimb, and process a tree into pulpwood length in about one minute. This machine, which International Paper Company engineers helped to design, is operated by one man. It can thin the rows of plantations as well as clearcut when the plantation is mature. (*Courtesy International Paper Co.*)

As we have mentioned, trees absorb carbon dioxide and release oxygen. This is a vital part of the growth process. During rain storms, the forest acts as a sponge, soaking up the water, using what it needs, and allowing the rest to filter back through the ground and into rivers, lakes, and other bodies of water. This same action would also be true of melting snow.

Note examples of selective cutting in Figures 2-4 and 2-5. Tree stumps are visible as evidence of the cuts.

Pleasing as this result may be to the public eye, however, there are also disadvantages. Since this method involves a tree stand of varying

Figure 2-4. Improvement cut in Francis Marion National Forest, South Carolina. (*Courtesy U.S. Forest Service*)

ages, there will be many trips into the forest to cut new trees as they mature.

Economically, this method is more costly than cutting a whole given area, the method known as clearcutting (discussed below). Also, look again at the heavy-duty equipment in Figures 2-1, 2-2, and 2-3. As this equipment repeatedly goes into the forest to haul out mature trees, the land is scarred again and again. Where young trees might have taken root in the scarred area, the tractor-driven vehicles crush everything in their path.

While in some methods of tree removal workers might delimb a

Figure 2-5. Selectively cut stand of shortleaf and loblolly at Bankhead National Forest, Alabama. (*Courtesy U.S. Forest Service*)

tree and haul it over the ground to a waiting truck, quite often the tree is cut into shorter lengths for more practical removal, as shown in Figure 2-6.

Perhaps you are wondering at this point at what age a tree becomes mature and ready for harvest. The answer varies with species, climate, environment, and other factors. Some trees might mature in 30 years or less, while others will easily continue growing until they have passed their hundredth birthday. This is still another reason why forest management, planning for the present and future, is so vital.

Shelterwood Cutting

The next type of harvesting is known as the *shelterwood method*. This type of cutting is designed to leave about 12 or 13 trees per acre while the rest are removed. The purpose is to leave the standing

Figure 2-6. Log bucking at Scott's Northwest Woodlands Operations headquartered at Everett, Washington. (*Courtesy Scott Paper Co.*)

Figure 2-7. Shelterwood cutting. Enough trees have been harvested so that the shade-intolerant Douglas fir will regenerate itself. Enough trees have been left to provide a seed source and to protect seedlings from frost, which is frequently fatal. The logging residue has not yet been treated. After treatment and seedling establishment, the shelterwood trees will be removed. This system is being used increasingly in forest types where it is biologically and otherwise feasible. Photo taken at Mt. Hood National Forest, Oregon. (*Courtesy U.S. Forest Service*)

timber as sources for reseeding as well as to offer a method of shelter for young seedlings (see Figure 2-7). When these seedlings have grown sufficiently, the shelter trees will be removed so that the new trees will have a clear area for growth.

As indicated in the illustration with Douglas fir, this type of tree requires sunlight for growth. If old trees are left standing too long, by virtue of their height they will shut out sunlight, which is vital to the healthy growth of the younger trees. Likewise, consider a light rain. If the overhead cover of a stand of trees is heavy, the rain will be intercepted by the the taller trees, depriving the younger and shorter trees of much needed moisture.

Seed Tree Method

Another harvesting pattern is known as the *seed tree method*. This resembles the previous method somewhat, in that about five or six trees per acre are left standing while the rest of the area is cut down. The procedure is used as a natural reseeding situation. In this case shelter is not the important aspect—only the regrowth of the forest area that has been harvested matters. An example of this is shown in Figure 2-8.

As you may have surmised, different species of trees and their

Figure 2-8. The area shown here was a mature stand of loblolly pine, which was cut down, leaving only seed trees standing. The timber removed was used both as pulpwood and saw-timber. This photo was taken in the Francis Marion National Forest, South Carolina. (*Courtesy U.S. Forest Service*)

Figure 2-9. Clearcutting in strips, an example in the true fir type in California. Timber like this is not suited to selective cutting because of stand decadence and the possibility of understory infection by dwarf mistletoe. After the young trees in the clearcut strips grow to seed-bearing age, the adjacent old-growth trees can be clearcut in strips. Tahoe National Forest, California. (*Courtesy U.S. Forest Service*)

environment, climate, and other factors will dictate the proper system of regrowth. Again, this is a vital aspect of proper forest management.

Although we have shown illustrations from the U.S. Forest Service of the different types of harvest, this same practice goes on throughout the forest products industry. As we stated earlier, private industry practices silviculture to a more serious extent, obtaining a greater yield of cubic feet of wood per acre of land (see Figures 1-1 and 1-2).

An area lacking proper management is that of the independent owner or tree farmer. Many small owners are not as knowledgeable as the professional forester, and therefore have left trees to grow in nature's own way. This picture is slowly changing as they accept assistance and advice from the woodlands department of the forest products industry, federal and state agencies. Since they derive revenue from the amount of wood harvested (expressed both by cubic feet and board feet), it is to their advantage to have a greater wood yield per acre of ground.

Thinning

One of the methods of increasing yield is to remove trees that are growing too close to one another (i.e., *thinning*). This will allow the standing trees to grow faster, taller, and healthier. When trees grow too close together, there is competition among them for the nutrients of the soil as well as water and sunlight, especially when they have grown sufficiently to have a broad overhead cover. When left alone, many of the young trees die because of this competition, which is one of nature's ways of survival of the fittest.

Clearcutting

Now we come to the most controversial type of timber harvest—*clearcutting*. There has been much clamor by the general public about clearing a whole area at one time. Admittedly, this yields an eyesore at first; but in years to come, the healthy regrowth of the forest is most beneficial. Economically, it is the most practical method of harvest whenever the area lends itself to this type of tree cutting. A forest crew with accompanying heavy-duty equipment comes into the area once and does its job. The area is now clear for reseeding, and the new growth will result in an *even-age* stand.

Clearcutting is far from new—it has been practiced for centuries throughout the world. Foresters in both private industry and the national forest service agree that it is the preferred harvesting procedure. It is the perfect solution to the mature area and allows management to control new growth. As young trees spring up, they can be thinned out so as to leave room for growth of the sturdier species.

Clearcutting in Strips

Note Figure 2-9, clearcutting in strips in a fir tree area in California. When the young seedlings are old enough to become seed-bearing, adjacent old growth will be cut.

An interesting example of clearcutting is shown in Figure 2-10. Note that the areas are staggered and irregular in a stand of old-growth Douglas fir. The reseeding will be done by nature—from the trees adjacent to the patches.

Figure 2-10. Clearcutting by staggered settings in old-growth Douglas fir. This method seeks to obtain full crop utilization with provision for adequate seed supply from adjacent timber for restocking the harvest area. Willamette National Forest, Oregon. (*Courtesy U.S. Forest Service*)

To pose another problem, what are some possible answers to an insect epidemic such as the spruce budworm that plagued the state of Maine in 1975–1976? Fighting the infestation with chemicals is one answer, but not a complete one because of the vast area involved. Setting fire to a large forest area to kill the insects might be another, but a most dangerous one because of the difficulty of control. Where all else fails, premature harvesting by clearcutting might help salvage much of the wood before it becomes totally unusable. Each situation is different, and a combination of the above solutions is undoubtedly the answer.

Advantages of Clearcutting

Let us consider a few pros and cons of this important method of wood harvesting. Here are some advantages of clearcutting:

1. Damage to the area is minimized because wood-cutting equipment does the entire job at one time.
2. In cleared areas, shrubs and plants that are desirable food for wildlife will grow. Wild game also finds such areas desirable because sunlight warms the area.
3. Tree blowdown is minimized because of the clearing.
4. Disease infestation is minimized. Young, healthy, growing trees, in most cases planted by the forest industries, are superior to their older predecessors and are better able to withstand the ravages of nature.
5. Rain water, which may have been intercepted by the overhead cover of an older stand, now reaches the ground.
6. Young trees do not have to compete with older trees for sunlight because they are shorter.
7. Logging a whole area at once yields more cubic feet of wood in a lesser period of time. This is important for the eventual pricing of wood products to the consumer.
8. Since it is now possible to grow supertrees in comparison to old-growth timber, new trees, with proper management, will have a greater yield per acre of land.

Figure 2-11. This mature forest was logged in the early 1930s. The area is on Willow Creek and was acquired by the Forest Service in 1938. Trees were planted in 1939 and 1942. St. Joe National Forest, Idaho. (*Courtesy U.S. Forest Service*)

Tree Growth Sequence at Willow Creek

Before enumerating some of the disadvantages, let us now observe some interesting photos from the Willow Creek area in the St. Joe National Forest, Idaho.

First, there is the basic photograph by the U.S. Forest Service where the area was clearcut, Figure 2-11. This is followed by a picture taken of the same area six years later, Figure 2-12. Young trees have begun to sprout. In Figure 2-13, the same scene is shown 11 years after the photo in Figure 2-11 was taken. The regrowth is now substantial. In Figure 2-14, 16 years have passed and the area has been well filled in with solid growth. The final photo in the series shows a flourishing forest 21 years later (Figure 2-15).

Figure 2-12. View of clearcut logging area on Willow Creek, 6 years after the photo in Figure 2-11 was taken. Note the young trees coming in. (*Courtesy U.S. Forest Service*)

Disadvantages of Clearcutting

Some of the disadvantages of clearcutting are as follows:

1. The area immediately cleared is an eyesore until new growth takes hold.
2. Climate control is not as good, leaving hotter days in the summer and colder days in the winter.
3. Watershed control is disrupted, since the trees have been cut down.
4. Unless it is properly planned, soil erosion might result.

Speaking of soil erosion, what would be the effect of clearcutting on mountain slopes? This is a serious matter, since melting snow and heavy rainfall can quickly erode the area if there is no watershed control. At the same time, trees will mature on mountain slopes just as they do on level ground. The same problem holds true for insect infestation. Yet if it is left to nature's solution, insects, blowdown, and fire will surely result to clear the area. Again we see the importance of forest management, evaluating each area for its own unique solution.

Figure 2-13. View of clearcut logging area on Willow Creek 11 years after the photo in Figure 2-11 was taken. (*Courtesy U.S. Forest Service*)

Figure 2-14. View of clearcut logging area on Willow Creek 16 years after the photo in Figure 2-11 was taken. (*Courtesy U.S. Forest Service*)

Access roads are another always important element in forest control as well as management. It would also be an unfortunate waste to leave trees in a mature state, unharvested.

In Figure 2-16, note the ground slope of the clearcut area, which was mature timber, mostly hemlock, in the Coeur d'Alene National Forest, Idaho.

Tree Nurseries

The final phase of our foresty program is to plant seeds in a nursery that will become the seedlings necessary for new growth. This can be done in greenhouses or in open fields, as shown in the photos in the following pages.

The growth of seedlings will also be affected by environmental factors: water, light, temperature, and the conditions best for the growth of each type of tree. In the forest there are some species that grow best in burnt-over land.

A discussion at a recent forest tree seedling symposium brought out the fact that growth of pine seedlings was approximately doubled when incandescent light was added to fluorescent light. Regarding temperature, optimum temperatures for growth were stated to be

Figure 2-15. View of clearcut logging area on Willow Creek 21 years after the first photo, Figure 2-11, was taken. (*Courtesy U.S. Forest Service*)

Figure 2-16. General view of clear cut on Solitaire Creek logging area. The mature timber, mostly hemlock, was logged in the Coeur d'Alene National Forest, Idaho. (*Courtesy U.S. Forest Service*)

20° to 25°C, or between 65° and 77°F with a temperature drop during the night. This might be compared to a comfortable temperature range in the month of September at a location such as Washington, D.C.

Seeding

` The following photos illustrate some of the methods of seeding. In Figure 2-17 a seed bed former is going over the ground. In Figure 2-18, conifer seedbeds are planted, contour-shaped, to conform to the area. In Figure 2-19, there is drill sewing of white pine seed. Note how effectively and quickly the job can be done with machinery designed for the purpose.

Figure 2-20 shows large rows of ponderosa pine in a tree seedling nursery after one year of growth. Some species will grow faster than others. The rate is also influenced, as we have stated earlier, by the amount of water, temperature, soil conditions, and climate. Quite often liquid fertilizer is also pumped into the water supply where it is deemed best.

In Figure 2-21, we see a transplanting of white spruce, which grows very slowly. It will take another two years of growth before this species will be ready for replanting into the forest.

Figure 2-17. Forming a seedbed with a Planet bed former at Jackson County nurseries in Indiana. (*Courtesy U.S. Forest Service*)

Figure 2-18. Conifer seedbeds planted on contour protected by mutiflora rosa (left) and Oriental arbovitae (right) windbreaks, in Norman, Oklahoma. (*Courtesy U.S. Forest Service*)

Figure 2-19. Drill sewing white pine seed at Savenac Nursery, Coeur d'Alene National Forest, Idaho. (*Courtesy U.S. Forest Service*)

Figure 2-20. Rows of one-year-old Ponderosa pine seedlings at Coeur d'Alene Nursery, Idaho. (*Courtesy U.S. Forest Service*)

Despite all of the nursery planting shown, in many areas tree farmers still rely on nature to reseed an area in a natural way.

There is no single answer to a given problem. However, we can draw some conclusions from the facts given in these two chapters. One, we know that we must harvest more wood for a growing population and a growing economy. Two, we also agree that a higher yield per acre of ground is required. Three, we must look upon our public forest lands as an adjunct to those of private industry so that the mature forest will be harvested commercially rather than destroyed naturally.

Figure 2-21. White spruce seedlings being transplanted at the U.S. Forest Service Chitten-don Nursery in Michigan. Young spruce seedlings grow very slowly. Here two-year-old seedlings are being transplanted so that they will have more room to grow for the next two years before they are planted in the forest. The machines are motor-driven and guided down the rows by a flanged wheel riding on an iron pipe. Crewmen ride backwards while transplanting seedlings. (*Courtesy U.S. Forest Service*)

The last-mentioned item is one which demands action by our legislators in Washington. We hope that this brief description of the forest and silvicultural possibilities will better educate the reader as to the forest problem and the solutions thereto.

3
PAPERMAKING

In the preceding chapters we discussed the problem of the forest, its maintenance, harvesting, management, and growth. Our next step is to get the wood to the mill for processing.

Log Transportation

In earlier years, one of the most economical ways of transporting logs was to float them down a river to the mill site. This gradually gave way to more modern means of transportation, particularly by rail and truck. Even so, the practice continued into the 1970s, when concern for the environment doomed water transport.

Today, paper mills use the railroads extensively, both for hauling logs to the mill and for transporting finished paper to the consumer. In Figure 3-1 we find an excellent example of logs loaded on flat cars at International Paper Company's Panama City, Florida, mill.

Transportation of raw material is a costly factor to every mill; it puts serious limitations on how far the mill can go to secure its raw wood for pulping. The ever increasing cost of motor fuel puts an additional strain on costs of transportation and is an important factor in paper prices to the consumer.

Figure 3-1. Trainloads of pulpwood are checked at International Paper Company's Panama City, Florida, mill. A steady flow of pulpwood to these large pulp and paper mills keep hundreds of people working in the woods each day. Pulpwood is also brought in by trucks from nearby areas. (*Courtesy International Paper Co.*)

Chipping

Another method of securing raw wood is to reduce the log to chips right in the forest. Chipping in the forest has many advantages. Instead of limbs and branches being left behind where they may become a fire hazard, these small units can now be utilized as pulp wood. There are whole-tree chippers, which lift up the entire tree, swallow it at one end, and spew chips into a waiting truck at the other end. This means that the usable tree yield is greater than it would be if only the trunk were utilized. Also, the loading time and cutting of logs into smaller units can be eliminated, thereby decreasing costs.

There are a few disadvantages to this operation. In the swallowing of the whole tree, the bark, which is undesirable for pulping, is also ground up into chips. This causes darker and dirtier pulp and makes the bleaching problem more difficult. Nevertheless, the disadvantage is overcome by the greater yield of the whole tree.

Getting back to the mill, let us see what happens after the wood leaves the forest.

Figure 3-2 is a picture of the Boise Cascade Corp. wood yard. On the left is a large pile of cut logs, while on the right is a sizable mound of wood chips. We should not assume that the logs will be converted into chips—that may or may not be true.

Debarking

In processing the logs, the first step is to remove the unwanted bark. Generally the wood bolts are transported to the wood room in

Figure 3-2. Wood yard at Boise Cascade Corp., Rumford, Maine. Logs awaiting processing are on the left, while the wood chip pile is on the right. (*Courtesy Boise Cascade Corp.*)

waste water from the bleaching area, a process which tends to soften the bark for easier removal. Then the bolts are transported by conveyor to huge slatted steel cylinders called barking drums. Here the logs roll and tumble against each other, and the bark is loosened and stripped from the log. Another method of stripping bark is using powerful jets of water against the logs, a procedure which also strips the unwanted areas from the bolts.

At this point, the debarked logs can go either to the chipper or the grinding room, depending upon the papermaking process. Let us start with the groundwood mechanical pulping process, the quick method of reducing the wood to a pulp by grinding.

Groundwood Pulping

In the most widely used mechanical method, the *stone groundwood* method, the logs are usually cut to four-foot lengths as an initial step before going into the debarking area. This size corresponds to the width of the grinding stones, which, as their name implies, grind the logs to a pulp in large quantities of water. The groundwood pulp is used primarily for newsprint and other fine printing papers that specify a groundwood content (generally less than 50%).

One disadvantage of groundwood pulping is that the grinding and crushing of fibers weakens them so that they are not nearly as strong as their chemically free counterparts. For this reason, newsprint is composed of approximately 80% groundwood and 20% chemical fibers intermixed for strength. The greatest advantage of this process is that the wood is fully utilized, including its impurities, to give greater yield.

At this point you should know some of the differences between hardwoods and softwoods. Hardwoods have shorter fibers and are more dense. Softwoods have longer fibers, are less dense, and therefore grow quicker. Obviously groundwood pulping would favor softwood because the fibers are longer.

Refiner Groundwood

In recent years a new method of making mechanical pulp has been developed, known as the *refiner groundwood* method. This process resulted from the greater availability of wood residues from sawmills and other sources, which are now converting wood residues into chips. The chips are fed into the refiners where they are reduced to fiber and fiber fragments in a series of attrition, or disc, mills.

The result is that we now have types of mechanical or groundwood pulp with different characteristics, even though they are used in similar grades. The mechanically ground pulp, or "stone groundwood," is weaker than refiner pulp but has more opacity and brightness. The refiner pulp, on the other hand, is stronger and bonds together better. As a result, the refiner groundwood process will make it possible to use even more hardwoods, preferably those that are less dense, like aspen or poplar.

Statistically, the production of groundwood is now in the vicinity of 5 million tons per year in the United States.

Semichemical Pulp

Another method of fiberization is the *semichemical* pulp method. As the name implies, there is some chemical treatment of the wood chips with cooking liquor to partially delignify the wood before sending it to the refiners for full fiberization. The full chemical treatment is discussed later in this chapter.

Thermomechanical Pulp

Another variation of mechanical pulp which has become quite popular is *thermomechanical* pulp. Once again the name is partly descriptive of the method, by indicating a heat process. A result of the availability of wood chips in increasing quantities, this process softens wood chips by the use of steam. While the wood has been soft-ened and is still heated, it is pumped into the refiners where fiberiza-tion takes place.

Figure 3-3. The paper industry uses billions of tiny wood chips annually. In preparation for chemical pulping, logs are debarked and reduced to chips, which range in size from $\frac{1}{2}$ to $\frac{3}{4}$ of an inch square and about $\frac{1}{8}$ inch thick. All chips are "screened" through a wire mesh for acceptability of size. Those found acceptable are sent on a conveyer belt to the pulp mill. Oversized chips are rechipped and returned again for a screening. Undersized chips are usually used as fuel in power boilers to help supply energy for the pulp and papermaking process. (*Courtesy Westvaco*)

As you can see, each process offers some advantages in converting raw wood to paper fibers. While the fine-paper-manufacturing segment of the paper industry mostly favors chemical pulp, a very large segment of printing paper is newsprint. In making stone groundwood papers we have had to add chemical fiber for strength. With new types of refiner groundwood, it may not be as necessary to add as much chemical pulp for strength as we have added heretofore. The impact would be even greater for industrial-type paperboard.

Fiber Length

Another interesting statistic is the size of the wood fibers we have been discussing. These fibers are thinner than a human hair. The length, on the other hand, varies from 1 to 2 millimeters in the case of hardwoods, from 3 to 6 millimeters for softwoods. Cotton fibers, on the other hand, are much longer and range up to about 25 millimeters. (There are 25 millimeters to the inch.)

Chemical Pulp

The next type of pulp is called *chemical pulp.* It is obtained by removing lignin and other impurities from the wood by a cooking process.

The cooking process requires wood chips. There is a similarity to making mashed potatoes: You can drop the potatoes whole into a pot of boiling water after removing the skin (the bark in the case of wood), but they would take longer to cook that way. A cook cuts the potatoes into small units because the cooking process is quicker. The papermaker also wants quicker results, so, in a similar fashion, he reduces the log into small chips to facilitate the cooking.

If the wood is to be chemical pulp, the wood bolts must be converted to chips. In this case, after debarking, the wood would continue along a conveyor into a "chipper." This is a log-swallowing device that has sharp steel blades. When the logs drop into the chipper, the rotating knives bite into the wood with a grinding noise, and in seconds the wood is cut into small units about $\frac{1}{8}''$ thick and roughly

Figure 3-4. Special custom-built truck unloading wood chips that have been precut away from the mill at Muskegon, Michigan. The truck drives onto a special platform, the front end is raised about 60°, and gravity unloads the vehicle into an underground hopper. Pneumatic tubes then transport the chips and empty them into a waiting chip pile. (*Courtesy S. D. Warren Co.*)

$\frac{1}{2}''$ to $\frac{3}{4}''$ square. (See Figure 3-3.) The chips fall into another conveyor belt, and sawdust and shives are screened out. The rest can be transferred onto a chip pile such as the one shown in Figure 3-2.

Chipping Waste Wood

Fortunately, the lumber industry decided recently that it was good business to convert its waste lumber into chips right on its premises. This is done by feeding unusable lumber cuts from the sawing process (slabs, edgings, etc.) into a chipper, which accepts the waste wood at one end and blows the chips into a waiting truck at the other end. Figure 3-4 shows a typical situation, wherein the waiting truck brings its load to the mill. A special unloading platform tilts the front end upwards about 60°, and the chips fall into an underground hopper. Pneumatic tubes then transport the chips and expel them into a waiting chip pile, as in Figure 3-5.

The next step is to load the chips into a digester, add cooking liquor, and, by pressure cooking, separate the wood fibers from other unwanted ingredients, principally lignin.

Figure 3-5. Wood chips blown into an open-air storage pile at S. D. Warren Company, Westbrook, Maine. (*Courtesy S. D. Warren Co.*)

Lignin

Lignin may be described as the glue that holds the fibers of the wood together in tree form. The lignin is also responsible for rapid discoloration of paper, such as in newsprint. It is dissolved in the chemical cooking process. When the cooking is done, the fibers then pass into the blow tank, after which they undergo both a washing and a bleaching phase. Many mills still use batch digesters, in which a load of chips is cooked and emptied out into the blow tank, after which another load is fed in to repeat the cycle.

Figure 3-6. At the Hammermill Pulp Mill, the wood chips are fed into a continuous digester where they are cooked under pressure and reduced to fiber form. (*Courtesy Hammermill Paper Co.*)

Continuous Digester

A more efficient method is to use a continuous digester, as shown in Figure 3-6. As the name implies, the process is continuous, permitting an uninterrupted flow of chips to pass through the cooking cycle without the delays encountered in loading and unloading the batch digesters. The diagram in Figure 3-7 shows a control panel for monitoring the action of another digester at the Boise Cascade Corp. mill in Rumford, Maine.

Figure 3-7. Softwood digester control panel at Boise Cascase Corp., Rumford, Maine. Softwood chips are cooked in a continuous flow digester, which produces 200 tons of soft-wood kraft pulp per day. (*Courtesy Boise Cascade Corp.*)

For the following description, as well as the diagram in Figure 3-8, we are indebted to the Kamyr Corporation:

In continuous pulping (as opposed to batch pulping) chips are fed in a continuous stream, mixed with cooking liquor, heated under pressure, and then washed to remove spent liquor and lignin from the pulp. The spent liquor-lignin mixture is then concentrated and

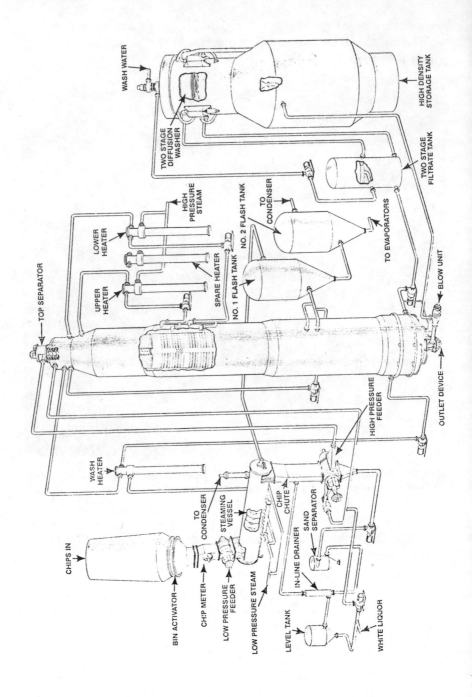

burned in a chemical recovery furnace to generate steam used in the process for "cooking" the chips, while the chemicals are recovered for reuse in the cooking-liquor cycle.

Chip Flow

The chip flow is as follows. Chips are conveyed to a *chip bin*, where steam is introduced to heat the chips to approximately 190°F. They are metered out of the bin by a *chip meter* and then transferred to a *steaming vessel* by a rotary lock called a *low pressure feeder*. This feeder isolates the pressurized steaming vessel from the atmosphere. In the steaming vessel the air is driven out of the chips by raising the temperature to 240°F, which enables the cooking liquor to impregnate the chips. The chips drop from the steaming vessel into a *high pressure feeder*, which isolates the digester and the steaming vessel.

The chips and liquor are mixed as the chips are pumped to the top of the digester. The top section of the digester is pressurized to 160 psi, and as the chip mass passes downward, the cooking liquor is penetrating into the chips. After about 45 minutes, the chips have passed through the *impregnation zone* and reach the *heating zone*, where hot liquor (340°F) is recirculated through the chips for heating.

The actual pulping (delignification) occurs at 335°F in about 90 minutes, a period which is the *cooking zone*. After passing through the cooking zone, the chips (which have now become pulp) are washed with weak liquor from washing stages that follow.

The pulp is continuously blown from the digester to the *diffusion washer*, where the washing of the pulp is completed.

The total time elapsed, from the time a chip enters the chip bin until it leaves the digester as pulp, is about five hours. Modern systems are now in operation that produce in excess of 1,500 tons of pulp

Figure 3-8. Schematic illustration of Kamyr Hydraulic Digester with Two-Stage Diffusion Washer, on opposite page.

per day from a single unit. These units are operated by a single operator and use about one-half the steam and one-third the power of older-type systems.

Chemical Free Pulp

The chemical pulp that emerges accounts for only about half of the starting material. The lignin and other carbohydrates account for the difference. The reason we use the expression "about half" is that the actual percentage of pure cellulose wood fibers will vary somewhat depending upon the type of wood being processed and the degree of cooking. In like manner, the amount of lignin also varies, but we can assume a general average of about 30%. To account for the balance, we might say that 16% of the wood represents carbohydrates, while the remaining 4% contains proteins, fats, resins, turpentine, and even more items in very small quantities.

If you are a newcomer to the paper industry, you might be wondering why all that hard work is necessary to reduce the wood to pure fibers, losing half of it in the manufacturing process. Our purpose in manufacturing chemical pulp is mainly to extract lignin. On exposure to light of any kind, the paper has a tendency to become yellowish, as you know from disposing of old newspapers. An additional factor is paper strength and longevity.

In the mechanical groundwood process, the crushing of fibers weakens them, owing to abrasion and shredding. For this reason, newsprint is made with the addition of some chemical pulp for added strength, while utilizing groundwood for pure economy. As time passes, this process may undergo another change. The refiner groundwood method offers a stronger pulp than its mechanical counterpart, although sacrificing some opacity in the process.

Sulfite and Sulfate

Briefly, we might also mention two processes of cooking which sound so much alike—sulfite and sulfate. The first is an acid process and not as popular now as it used to be. Some hardwoods may be dissolved with difficulty by the sulfite (acid) process. On the other hand, the sulfate process, commonly referred to as the kraft process, is alkaline and yields a stronger pulp; it is the preferred method in most mills. The sulfite process uses sulfur dioxide and lime. The sulfate process uses sodium hydroxide (caustic soda) and sodium sulfide. After the cooking process, most of the chemicals are recovered and reused.

The sulfate process is the best method, overall, for cooking hardwood pulp. It is also useful in cooking both hard- and softwood pulp together, which is advantageous because the long softwood fibers add strength, while the shorter hardwood fibers are useful for filling in the gaps to make a more even sheet of paper. This process also improves paper formation, surface smoothness, and printability.

Figure 3-9. Brown stock, similar to a grocery bag in color, emerges from a washing and cleaning system. From here, the stock will go through a four-stage bleaching process. After each stage, dissolved impurities are washed from the pulp. (*Courtesy S. D. Warren Co.*)

Cooking Liquor

Another important item is recovery of the cooking liquor. An evaporation process is used to separate the spent chemicals and the dissolved wood impurities. The liquors become thick and are sprayed into a furnace. Here the wood material burns and is valuable in generating steam for the papermaking process. The ash from the cooking liquor fuses into a pool and from there to a dissolving tank. This recovery is advantageous in two ways: (1) the cooking chemicals are reused, and (2) the spent chemicals are *recycled* instead of being discharged into a body of water, thereby avoiding water pollution.

Figure 3-10. This four-stage bleaching operation at Hammermill Paper Company removes the natural brown coloring of the wood pulp and prepares it for the paper mill. (*Courtesy Hammermill Paper Co.*)

Bleaching

The washing of the fibers is done in several steps, as well as screening (see Figure 3-9). The next stage is bleaching. This, too, is done in several successive steps. A four-stage bleaching process would entail chlorination, caustic soda, sodium hypochlorite, and chlorine dioxide. By the end of the last treatment, the fibers are converted from a brownish mass to a pleasing white substance.

In Figure 3-10 we have an overhead view of the bleaching process at Hammermill Paper Company. Figure 3-11 shows a similar process at Boise Cascade from a side view.

Figure 3-11. Bleach plant at Boise Cascade Corp., Rumford, Maine. The four-stage process subjects the pulp to chlorination in the first phase, caustic extraction in the second, hypochlorite in the third, and chlorine dioxide in the fourth. (*Courtesy Boise Cascade Corp.*)

Blending Fibers

Despite the elaborate process of fiber separation and bleaching, we are not yet ready to form the paper on the "wet end" of the machine. We like to use softwood fibers for strength, hardwood fibers for fine quality. Blending the two together for the manufacture of fine printing papers in various proportions is a common procedure, depending on the type of sheet to be made.

Refiners

In order to prepare the fibrous slurry for better formation in our fine printing papers, we put them through a series of refiners. The fibers are actually hollow and stiff, so they are put through a series of serrated metal discs in the refiners, which then rough them up, fray them, and cause the fibers to collapse. This gives the mixture better bonding quality, allowing the fibers to adhere to each other more advantageously at the wet end of the process.

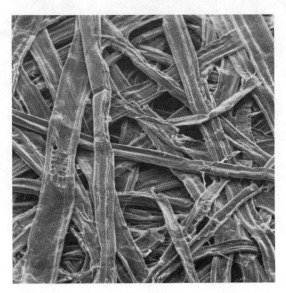

A

Figure 3-12.

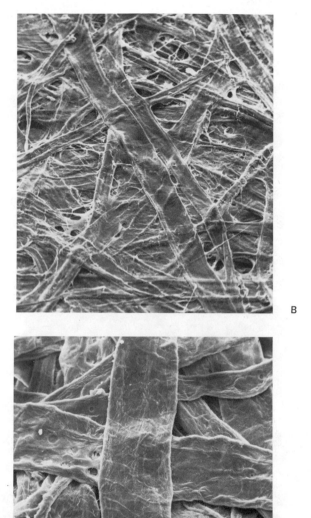

B

C

Figure 3-12.

Electron Micrographs

We are indebted to Dr. R. A. Parham of the Institute of Paper Chemistry for four scanning electron micrographs (Figure 3-12), which show the condition of the fibers before and after refining.

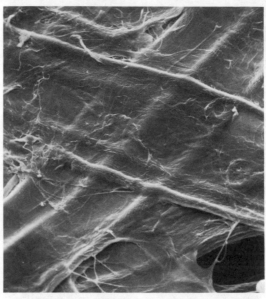

D

Figure 3-12. (A) An unrefined (unbeaten) kraft, softwood pulp. SEM (scanning electron micrograph). 110X. (B) Same pulp as in "A," after 50 minutes of beating. SEM. 110X. (C) Intersection of collapsed but unbeaten fibers of Southern Pine Earlywood. SEM. 440X. (D) Similar fiber intersection as in "C" except in beaten pulp. SEM. 660X. Four photos: from *An Atlas of Electron Micrographs* by R. A. Parham and Hilkka M. Uaustinen, (Institute of Paper Chemistry.)

Fine printing papers must possess many qualities to reproduce the printed word and photograph in a suitable manner, not the least of which is trouble-free press performance. There are still hills and valleys that must be evened out. Even though the fibers have been carefully washed, screened and bleached in a series of steps, the degree of whiteness may not yet be adequate. Or, perhaps a more creamy shade is preferred for book papers. Then there is a wide range of colors that each mill features in different grades.

Additives

Additives represent the next step in our papermaking process. The hills and valleys we mentioned above are evened out somewhat by the addition of fillers such as clay and calcium carbonate. Besides acting as fillers, they also tend to add brightness to paper. These additives must be finely ground so as not to form lumps, which will pick off and raise havoc on a printing press. The problem of properly bonding fibers, intermixed with fillers and other chemical additives such as dyes and pigments, as well as sizing, is a problem of

Figure 3-13. Pulps are mixed together in blenders with other papermaking materials such as dyestuffs, sizing, and fillers, to produce the desired color and characteristics in the finished product. (*Courtesy Hammermill Paper Co.*)

constant research in the graphic arts industry. The basic printing processes of letterpress, lithography, and gravure have one set of standards when printing is from sheets, but there are different forms of stress when printing is from rolls. We are also concerned with the problems of ink holdout, tear strength, printability, pick resistance, water resistance (particularly in lithography), bulk, and color (especially the many shades of white).

Some other fillers besides those mentioned are titanium dioxide, barium sulfate, and zinc sulfide. The titanium filler is an important additive for giving exceptional whiteness to paper and is commonly used in paper classified as white opaque. Sizing is used mostly in lithographic papers to give water resistance. This additive is not necessary in letterpress or gravure. Others requiring sizing are bond, writing, kraft, and drawing papers. Figure 3-13 illustrates a "mixing tank" or blender where dyes and fillers are added.

Some mills do not make their own pulp but purchase it from other suppliers. When this is done, the pulp in dried sheets must be heavily diluted with water in some sort of container or tank and then go through finishing processes. First the pulp is churned and agitated so that the fibers separate. Then the fibers go through refiner action to beat and fray them for better bonding strength. Additives are then mixed into the pulp according to a predetermined plan, which brings the slurry or furnish to its desired state.

The Headbox

The makeready process is almost complete. The furnish is pumped into a headbox where it is now over 99% water. All of the elaborate preparations have been completed, and the next step is to place the stock onto a forming wire and remove practically all of the water to form paper.

The Fourdrinier

The opening in the headbox is called the "slice." At this point the stock, over 99% water, is released onto a rapidly moving wire mesh called the fourdrinier.   In this manner, we actually form paper for use in its many grades.

As the paper flows onto the *wire*, as it is commonly called, the fibers tend to form in the direction of flow.   While the fourdrinier moves rapidly forward, it also shakes or vibrates from side to side. This action is beneficial in that the fibers interlace with each other, while water, to some extent, falls through the wire mesh.   The draining of water is also assisted by suction boxes placed along the underside of the wire.   The objective is now to remove 95% of the water in the finished paper.

Simple as it may sound, many questions can be asked at this point. How fast is the fourdrinier moving?   How much stock is released through the slice, and how is this quantity controlled?   Since paper comes in various basis weights, how is this variable determined? These are but a few of the very important questions to be answered at this point.

To take the first question, of how fast the wire is moving, it seems that the answer varies with every mill making paper.   As an economic measure, it is desirable to manufacture the finished product in the least amount of time so as to minimize costs.   Some fourdrinier wires move at slow speeds of several hundred feet per minute—others move at speeds faster than 3,000 feet in the same amount of time.   The objective is to keep increasing the speed while maintaining the quality of the paper.

Another factor is the basis weight of the stock, which we shall discuss in a later chapter.   For now, we can say that the thickness of the paper is determined by the amount of furnish released from the headbox in relation to the speed of the wire.   This used to vary to some small extent from one processing batch to another.   Today, it is more scientifically measured and controlled by computer.

Obviously there are many variables in papermaking.

Another important factor in papermaking capacity is the width of the fourdrinier.   The wider the machine is, the more paper there can be formed per unit of time.   This is also important to the customer, who may be interested in buying carloads of paper at one time of a particular size or roll width.

Figure 3-14. Wet end of the paper machine. At this point in the papermaking process, the pulp, having been washed, refined and bleached, is pumped into a headbox, part of which appears in the lower left of the picture. The pulp, in the form of fibers suspended in water, leaves the headbox through a very narrow horizontal opening called a "slice." It then moves onto an endless, moving wire or "screen," where the sheet is actually formed when the fibers lock together. A series of metal rolls, located underneath the wet end wire, aids the drainage of water through the wire and away from the fibers. (*Courtesy Westvāco*)

Dandy Roll

Getting back to the fourdrinier, note the illustration in Figure 3-14. As the paper flows along the wire and water is drained along the way, a dandy roll near the end helps to smooth out the paper. It is not feasible to state exactly what percentage of water will remain at the end of the fourdrinier run because this will vary from one mill to another—principally because of the speed of movement of the wire.

While the principal purpose of the dandy roll is to improve the formation of the paper web by application of pressure, it is also a good point at which to place a watermark in wove or laid papers if desired. This is often done in better-quality bond papers, particularly rag bonds. Note the close-up view in Figure 3-15.

Figure 3-15. Close-up view of the suspended pulp fibers, still dispersed in about 99% water. In the photo the pulp is moving toward the dandy roll at the left. The dandy roll is a cylinder covered with very fine wires running both the circumference and the length of the cylinder and crossing each other at close intervals. At this point a watermark on the dandy roll can be imparted to the newly formed but still very moist sheet. (*Courtesy Westvāco*)

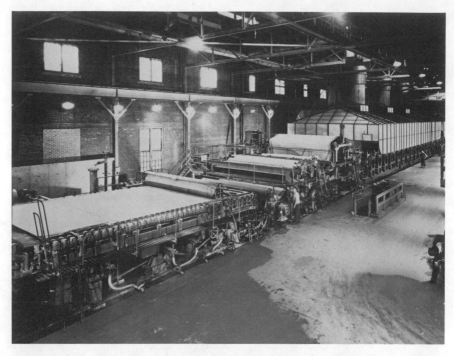

Figure 3-16. The stock, diluted with over 99% water, flows onto the fine mesh fourdrinier wire screen. While flowing toward the driers, the screen moves and shakes to weave and mat the fibers together as some of the water drains off. The paper travels nearly a quarter of a mile as it moves up, down, and around more than 50 drying drums. (*Courtesy Hammermill Paper Co.*)

As the paper web races across the fourdrinier, or wet end of the machine, it has been fully formed and now goes through the press and drying sections. When the paper reaches the end of the wire, it is transferred to a felt blanket which conveys it through many steam-heated driers to remove the excess moisture. Figure 3-16 shows an extended view of the paper web flowing from the wet to the dry end.

As the web winds up and over each set of drying drums, the water is evaporated in a huge cloud of steam. With each move from one dryer section to the other, the water content gets smaller and smaller until it reaches the final stage, leaving about 5% moisture in the paper.

Perhaps you are wondering why we take out only 95% of the water and not 100%. The reason is that if the paper were 100% dry, with no moisture content, it would be brittle and crack easily.

Figure 3-17 is a close-up view of the newly formed paper leaving the fourdrinier and entering the drying section.

Machine Coating

We have described the basic papermaking process so far, a system used by most mills with some moderate variations of one form or another. While the paper is in the drying section, other activities often take place. For example, sizing is often put on the paper after it goes through a series of drying drums, after which it continues through

Figure 3-17. Close-up view of paper leaving the wire and entering the press section of the paper machine. An endless "press felt" picks up the wet sheet at the couch roll and carries it into the "first press." Paper and felt pass between two press rolls, where excess water is squeezed out of the paper and into the felt. (*Courtesy S. D. Warren Co.*)

another series of press rollers before completing its journey. Another very important step is known as the machine coating process. When this is done, the base stock is thinner than it would be if the paper were to be, for example, uncoated offset. A coating is put on both sides of the paper, and, depending upon its grade, it continues through additional dryers, or even more coaters to obtain a desired finish. Figure 3-18 illustrates an on-the-machine coater.

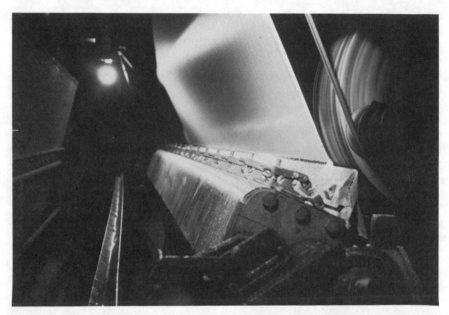

Figure 3-18. On-Machine Coaters at Warren's Westbrook mill. Paper coatings are pigments mixed with water and adhesives to form a thick, high-solids material resembling latex house paint. These are applied at one or more On-Machine Coaters and provide a printing surface superior to that of uncoated papers. Paper is redried between coating applications in additional dryer sections placed after each coater station. Size press, impregnation, and trailing blade coating are the three methods used on the paper machines. (*Courtesy S. D. Warren Co.*)

Calendering

Now that the paper has completed its manufacturing process and has received some coating or surface sizing as required, it passes through a series of calender stacks. The calender is a series of polished iron rollers, stacked one on top of the other, through which the finished paper will pass to be smoothed down. If the paper is to be smoothed down only lightly, giving it a vellum or "rough-feel" finish, it will pass through fewer rollers than a smooth-finish paper. This calendering process will affect the bulk of the paper but have no effect whatsoever on its basis weight. (See Figure 3-19.)

Rewinding

The next step is rewinding. After the paper has been calendered, it is wound on a metal or fiber core. Coated paper will generally be wound on a metal core because of its heavier weight. (See Figure 3-20.)

Following rewinding, there is a process of slitting rolls to a width specified by a customer. In most cases the rolls are shipped for use on a web press, either letterpress, offset, or gravure.

Figure 3-19. The paper machine process is almost complete as paper leaves the last bank of dryers and passes through the Machine Calender—a series of polished iron rollers stacked one on top of another. Bulk and surface finish are controlled partially by the number of passes between the iron rollers and also by varying calender pressures. The paper is wound under tension onto large reels. (*Courtesy S. D. Warren Co.*)

Figure 3-20. Paper rewinding.   After the paper has completed its journey through huge steam-heated drying drums, it passes through heavy steel calender rolls which help smooth and firm the surface. Then the paper is wound on a metal or hard paper core where it forms a roll weighing many tons. After this, the new roll is rewound for inspection and tightening up as shown in the photo. (*Courtesy Westvāco*)

Supercalendering

Another step in the process, which is sometimes used, is supercalendering. As its name implies, it is additional calendering to give paper an extrasmooth finish. This unit also has a stack of rollers, alternately metal and fiber-composition rolls. This additional smoothing operation compacts paper even more and is used to produce a very level, high-gloss finish to fine coated enamel papers, as shown in Figure 3-21.

Figure 3-21. Supercalender. Following the rewind step, and depending on its end use, the paper may be run through a supercalender. This unit, separate from the paper machine, consists of a series of alternately stacked metal and fiber-composition rolls. As the paper travels through the supercalender it is further compacted and smoothed, a process which produces a flat, glossy surface suitable for high-quality printing. (*Courtesy Westvāco*)

Many years ago supercalendering was used on unfinished, or uncoated, paper to give it a very smooth finish. This was prior to the popularity of machine-coated paper, when smoothness was a *must* for letterpress publications in order for them to accept halftones with some degree of fine screen and quality.

Sheeting

If the specifications call for sheeting to a given size, this is done in a sheeting department. This process is being constantly updated to

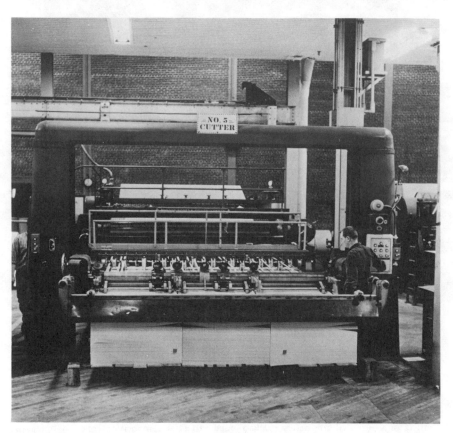

Figure 3-22. High-speed cutters sheet as many as eight rolls at one time. Trained inspectors sample the sheetfed production. (*Courtesy Hammermill Paper Co.*)

minimize the amount of labor. For example, Figure 3-22 shows rolls slit into three sheet piles. As many as eight rolls of paper can be fed into the machine and trimmed at the same time.

Figure 3-23 The AccuTrim® machine, developed by Westvaco Corporation, operates at speeds of 300 cuts per minute and automatically inspects, trims, cuts, sorts, counts, and stacks precision sheeted paper on a shipping skid. Sheeting is completed in one continuous operation, which eliminates the possibility of defects after inspection. (*Courtesy Westvaco*)

Another type of sheeter is the AccuTrim® machine of the Westvaco Corporation shown in Figure 3-23. This equipment operates at 300 cuts per minute and automatically inspects, trims, cuts, sorts, counts, and stacks on a skid.

Figure 3-24. Shipping warehouse. More than a million pounds of finished paper is stored in the mill warehouse, in rolls, skids, and cartons. Orders are assembled and loaded onto trucks or rail cars at special sidings. Individual orders can range from a single 150-lb carton to hundreds of tons of paper. (*Courtesy S. D. Warren Co.*)

Packing

Packaging of the finished paper is another important item. If it is packed on skids, the paper must be thoroughly wrapped and strapped, with identification labels placed on it. A label will give such vital statistics as the name, size, basis weight, and amount of paper, as well as other information. In conformity with the recent decision to switch to the metric system eventually, metric sizes and weights will be given as well as the conventional dimensions in inches and weights in pounds. This subject will be covered in greater detail in Chapter 7.

If the paper is to be packed in cartons, the same type of label identification will be used. In Figure 3-24 we show typical warehouse storage of paper.

Testing

Papermaking is far from being a routine business. Every mill has a research and testing department constantly to monitor the output for quality control. Every sheet has certain characteristics peculiar to its grade and basis weight. Some of the items tested are opacity, strength, whiteness, uniformity, color, specified basis weight, and a host of other standards. In Figure 3-25 we have one example using chemicals. In Figure 3-26, testing is being done on a press in the print shop.

Figure 3-25. Research. Scientists and technicians are engaged in all phases of research: pulping, papermaking, coating, finishing, printing, inks, and many other items. (*Courtesy S. D. Warren Co.*)

Figure 3-26. Print shop. This is another form of quality control. Using regular presses and inks, paper is tested on a 24-hour basis. Limited research is conducted in the shop. Customer complaints or problems are also investigated there. (*Courtesy S. D. Warren Co.*)

Components in a Ton of Paper

An interesting sidelight is found in the question: what does it take to manufacture a ton of paper? While every grade of paper will have its variations, as well as formulation by the different paper mills, Nekoosa Papers Inc. offers these statistics:

Water	55,000 gallons
Sulfur	102 pounds
Magnesium hydroxide	94 pounds
Lime	350 pounds
Salt cake	80 pounds
Caustic	66 pounds
Starch	108 pounds
Wood	2 cords
Power	112 kilowatt hours
Coal	1.2 tons
Alum	61 pounds
Clay	289 pounds
Rosin	16 pounds
Dye and pigment	20 pounds

To the above items must be added the capital investment in machinery and the cost of labor. When these figures were compiled, Nekoosa estimated labor at 20 man-hours per ton.

Flow Chart

By way of a summary of what has been described in paper manufacture, Figure 3-27 shows a graphic presentation of the process, step by step, at the Westbrook mill of the S. D. Warren Company. Some of the items shown in the schematic diagram have been either not covered yet or treated lightly. For example, on the bottom of the left-hand page there is a pumping station that receives waste water from the manufacturing process. Note that the water gets both primary and secondary treatment before passing into the river. This is a form of environmental control to avoid water pollution. Although the river can "digest" or clean up a certain amount of waste, the effluent from a paper mill is generally greater than a body of water can absorb.

In the right center of the right-hand page, the embosser is a machine that accepts the finished paper and puts a pattern on it. This paper can be either coated or uncoated.

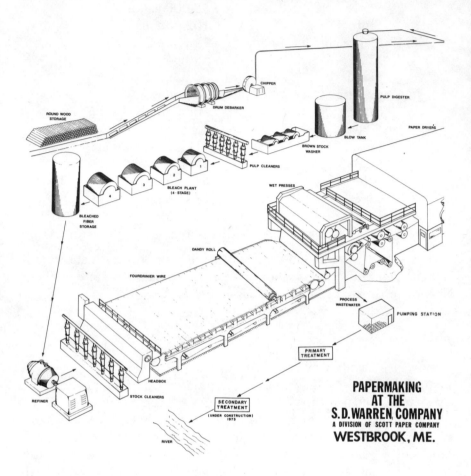

ROUND WOOD STORAGE

DRUM DEBARKER

CHIPPER

PULP DIGESTER

PAPER DRYERS

BLOW TANK

BROWN STOCK WASHER

PULP CLEANERS

BLEACH PLANT (4-STAGE)

4 3 2 1

WET PRESSES

BLEACHED FIBER STORAGE

DANDY ROLL

FOURDRINIER WIRE

PROCESS WASTEWATER

PUMPING STATION

PRIMARY TREATMENT

HEADBOX

STOCK CLEANERS

REFINER

SECONDARY TREATMENT
(UNDER CONSTRUCTION)
1973

RIVER

PAPERMAKING
AT THE
S.D.WARREN COMPANY
A DIVISION OF SCOTT PAPER COMPANY
WESTBROOK, ME.

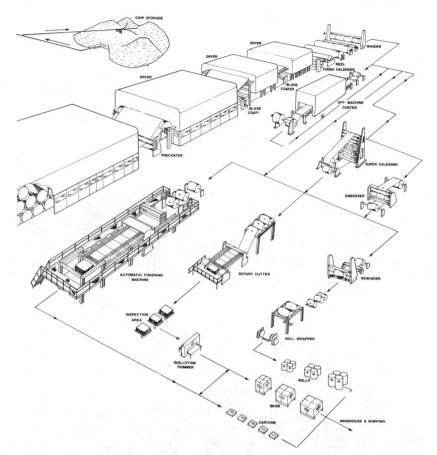

Figure 3-27. Schematic diagram of the papermaking process at S. D. Warren Company, Westbrook, Maine. This flow chart is typical of most types of fine printing papers, although fine coated paper is emphasized here.

Also on the right-hand page are two methods of sheeting paper. The process on the left is the more modern, using an automatic finishing machine. The older method, still being used, is to sheet several rolls at one time, using a machine trim. After inspection, the paper is then fed into a guillotine cutter, where it is trimmed on four sides. From here, the sheets are either stacked on skids or packed in cartons.

In the lower right, the paper is shipped directly to the customer or is placed in the warehouse from which future customer orders will be filled.

Twin Wire Machine

A recent breakthrough in the technology of papermaking is the twin wire machine, designed to replace the fourdrinier. Often we hear about the two-sidedness of paper—the felt side and the wire side, a characteristic of the fourdrinier. With the twin wire, both sides will be alike.

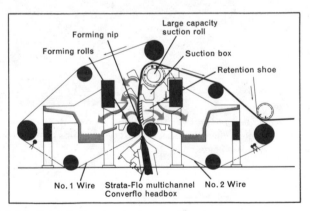

Figure 3-28. Beloit Bel Baie II twin wire former. The slurry passes from the headbox at the bottom center and passes between two forming rolls. At that point both no. 1 and no. 2 wires converge to carry the newly formed paper vertically upward, deflecting water rapidly, also aided by the suction box and suction roll. Note that the paper then follows the no. 2 wire to the right, then separates to continue through the dryer section.

Figure 3-28 is a schematic diagram of the Beloit Bel Baie II twin wire former. We have shown a diagram only, rather than the actual machinery, because it is easier to understand. Many other manufacturers make twin wire machines with different configurations and designs, but the principle of twin wire forming is basically the same.

The diagram in Figure 3-28 shows the paper moving vertically, as opposed to the horizontal formation of the fourdrinier. As the water shoots out of the headbox, it passes between two forming rolls and is carried between the two wires a very short distance, about several feet. In that short distance the paper is actually formed; water is deflected from both wires, aided also by a suction box and suction roll. The newly formed paper travels along the no. 2 wire, then continues on to the pressing and dryer sections.

There are many advantages claimed for this new system. For one, the two-sided paper is now eliminated. Another feature is the great flexibility of paper thickness, from tissue to board. The speed of formation is still another: even though the fourdrinier has attained speeds of 3,000 feet per minute, it is felt that 4,000 feet per minute is feasible for fine printing papers with twin wire equipment, or perhaps even more.

In conclusion, we have covered the basic papermaking process although we have not covered its many variations. For example, for text and writing papers there are special finishes used for the former, but mainly some rag content added to the latter.

Rag Content

When 25% or 50% rag is specified for a writing paper, it means that the balance of the fiber is wood. If a special finish, such as linen, is indicated, it has probably been formed by the dandy roll. On the other hand, text papers may have special finishes and textures created by marking felts, generally at the press section. This section is just beyond the fourdrinier and before the dryers.

Sometimes fancy finishes are created by feeding sheets of paper through special embossing machinery, an off-line process. In such cases the paper is very compressed, having low bulk for its basis weight.

4
PAPER—
HOW TO USE IT

Paper is the medium for printed communication. It comes in so many forms, sizes, colors (especially many shades of white), basis weights, finishes, and special characteristics, that it will be impossible to cover every usage. Nevertheless we shall try to cover the main areas with the hope that some of the descriptions will offer clues that the reader will find valuable.

Newsprint

The first type of paper is newsprint. All daily newspapers use this type because it is the most economical. Rarely does one quote the cost per pound—almost always it is cost per ton. Some newspapers use newsprint in sheets for letterpress printing, but they are the exception. Most often by far, newprint is fed from rolls, both in letterpress and offset, and sometimes by gravure.

Newsprint is mostly groundwood, which means it is subject to rapid discoloration on exposure to light of any sort. The grinding process of manufacture cuts the fibers, making the paper weak in terms of durability. Longer-fibered chemical pulp is added to the paper to give it some strength and durability.

Opacity is a very good feature of newsprint. All of the impurities of the wood, principally lignin, offer natural opacity without chemical additives. Another good feature is the bulk of this type of paper and the minimum need for bleaching.

Many publications use newsprint because it provides a printing surface that is printable, offers reasonable color, and permits the reproduction of both line work and halftones in all major printing processes. Since discoloration is one of the disadvantages, obviously it is used in publications where longevity is not an important factor.

Like other printing papers, newsprint can be whitened by the addition of bleaching agents. If more sizing is desired for some special purpose, this can also be done by the manufacturing mill. However, we must realize that special qualities require an order of sufficient tonnage to justify the making order. Some mills may accept as little as a carload (40,000 lb), but the amount may well vary with economic conditions and the backlog of orders on hand.

Colored Newsprint

Perhaps you should think in terms of colored newsprint. The yellow pages of the telephone directories are an excellent example. Other colors, such as blue and green are also common, and offer the advantage of hiding many of the impurities of the standard grayish-white sheet. Colored newsprint is still economical, although the additional dyes will justify a slightly increased cost.

Newspaper Webs

Another important consideration in using newsprint (mainly for economy) concerns the presses that print the paper. Since the stock is highly absorbent, and mostly printed on web presses, the simplest type of web is adequate. In fact, there is so much newsprint printed from rolls that I often refer to these presses as *newspaper webs*, to emphasize the use of a simple, economical printing press, as distinguished from a press that is designed mainly for finer printing papers.

Most newspaper web presses are designed for "soft folds" of both standard and tabloid sizes. Presses for daily newspapers have added features, such as the ability to print sections separately, then insert one inside the other at the delivery end. Once again, the advantage of this type of press is the ability to start with rolls of paper at one end and deliver the finished product at the other, without the necessity of using binding equipment to complete the package.

If you are puzzled by the terminology "soft folds," think of your daily newspaper—or better yet, pick one up and examine it. You will note that the folding edge is rounded. This is different from the commercial publication that requires a binding process to complete the product.

Offset Papers

The next line of printing paper in the uncoated field is offset paper, with a large differential in price from newsprint. How big a differential? Two to three times as much! This seems hard to believe, so perhaps a technical explanation might help.

Most offset papers are chemical-free sheets. This means, at the outset, that half of the wood pulp is lost in the making, or delignification, if you prefer. Then there is the cost of fillers and additives, sizing, extensive washing and bleaching, and more manufacturing time and man-hours. It all adds up.

One way to beat the high cost of offset papers, if you are looking for something less expensive in between, is to buy in sufficient quantity to justify your own manufacturing specifications. For example, taking a 40,000-lb carload as a minimum, you might specify a percentage of groundwood content. Perhaps you can do with less whiteness, less chemical additives. Another way to beat the whiteness factor is to add coloring dyes to give the paper an other-than-white shade (a tint of green, for example).

There is also the basis weight factor. You can always drop the weight and compensate for bulk by using more groundwood—which adds bulk naturally. At the end of the drying process, when the paper is being smoothed down by the calender stacks, the less the nip the greater the bulk. A word of caution, however, on the basis weight. Check with the mill manufacturer, probably through your local paper distributor, to find out how low you can drop in weight before adding a light-weight penalty. If the light-weight penalty is not too severe, balance that against your total postage or freight costs in the finished product, and make your decision.

Offset papers are mainly designed for the offset, or lithographing, printing process. This necessitates sizing to resist water, especially in sheet-fed printing. In web offset printing, the sizing can be minimal because of the high speed of press operation as well as the web tension during printing. All of these technical considerations add up to spelling out what *you* want in paper. After all, you're paying for it!

Offset papers have many uses. As the name indicates, the offset lithography printing process provides the prime use of the paper. But let your imagination run wild, and you will discover many other applications.

Paper Finish

Another use, for example, is letterpress. Type or line work is best in this case, because the offset papers generally have a somewhat rough finish. On the other hand, specify a smooth-finish offset for your purposes, and you'll get it. We mentioned type only because the letterpress process, printing directly from type or photoengravings, favors a smooth-finish paper, especially for halftones. If a rough-finish paper is used, the screen of the halftone would have to be coarse. A good example of this is the daily letterpress newspaper using a 65-screen halftone.

Mimeograph

Many people have found vellum-finish offset paper suitable for mimeographing. This is a declining process because of the economy of paper and paper-composition offset printing plates. These plates are ideal for short runs below 1,000 copies using type or line copy.

Letterheads are another use for offset stock. When the budget is tight, or the need for letterheads does not require a rag content, regular-finish offset paper fits very nicely. News or press releases are ideal for this situation, as are form promotion letters, catalog sheets, price lists, looseleaf inserts, to name but a few examples.

Offset Paper for Books

Books and other publications use offset papers in enormous quantities. Take books as an example. Some decades ago it was customary for books to be printed by letterpress. This meant holding many tons of letterpress type for anticipated reruns. When halftones were required, coated paper was used, but unfortunately it had to be a separate section. It was not feasible to print the photograph near the text because of mechanical limitations.

Today, the situation has changed. The lithography printing process has eliminated the need for holding letterpress type. Each page is photographed, and any necessary halftones are stripped into a desired position near the text which they illustrate. The paper is sized for the offset process, and 133-screen is average for this method of printing. For reruns, the stripped-up flats are held for future use, requiring relatively little space. If a page has to be changed, a new page can be made up or the correction made and the item photographed and stripped in place of the old copy. Remaking plates is quite inexpensive and normal.

Opaque Paper

Chemical additives also make a difference. If more whiteness is desired, more bleach can be added. If more opacity is desired, and whiteness is to be increased at the same time, an excellent additive is titanium. This paper has been given the separate classification of "opaque." A good example of its use is in higher-quality printed literature, such as annual reports. The added whiteness and opacity are excellent for printing process color.

Mimeo Papers

A brief word about mimeograph papers since they have been mentioned above. Although use of the process has greatly declined with the appearance of the offset short run plate, its advantage is that mimeograph machines are still easily used in a business office. The capital investment is small, compared to the cost and maintenance of the smallest offset press (such as the Multilith). The paper is more porous than the vellum-finish offset, thereby requiring less sizing in manufacture.

It may seem strange that the costs of mimeograph papers are a bit higher than the ordinary offset equivalent, despite less sizing. The explanation can only be that the mass-produced tonnage of offset papers brings the price lower.

Mimeo papers for office use are easily obtainable in the standard $8\frac{1}{2} \times 11$ or $8\frac{1}{2} \times 14$ inch sizes. Multiples of these sizes are available for commercial printing use. This is logical when you consider that many organizations using these papers can only reproduce their company logos, or perhaps add color to the usual black ink, by preprinting the paper in sizable quantities. The printer can then cut the sheets apart, usually to $8\frac{1}{2} \times 11$, and deliver them to the customer.

Tablet Paper

Of lesser known use, commercially, is tablet paper, an economical grade used for school purposes. Much of this type has a partial groundwood content for maximum economy. As you may expect, some sizing is introduced in manufacture to offer a better surface for ink writing. Bleaching is minimal.

Bond Paper

The next category is bond paper. The term came into being many years ago because this paper was used to print bonds and stocks. This is no longer true. Nevertheless, bond paper is a common item in business offices.

There are two principal types of bonds—sulfite and rag content. Let us discuss sulfite bonds first. The ordinary bond, used as typing paper mainly in business offices, is made from wood fiber. The sulfite process of manufacture may or may not be used, but that term for it still lingers, mainly to distinguish it from the type with rag, or cotton fiber, content.

Sulfite bonds are rated as No. 1 and No. 4 mainly. The numbers 2 and 3 have disappeared, and not even the memory lingers on. Although No. 1 is the better grade, the difference in cost from No. 4 is not very great. Most No. 1's are watermarked with the trade name. Also not too common is No. 5 bond, the lowest-price paper, but it is still available where cost is primary.

When shall we use bond papers? Mainly for typing. Colored bonds, generally yellow, are commonly used as office file copies of correspondence. After the typing use, perhaps the paper is also useful as a ruled school sheet. As a printing paper, there really is no limitation to its use. Bonds contain sizing to be useful for ink writing, which means that they will perform well on an offset printing press, or in letterpress printing if you prefer.

The sulfite bond has many characteristics which are similar to those of offset papers, so similar, in fact, that the day must come when the two shall merge into one category, perhaps using the name "offset bond" to bridge the gap. Bond papers are known as 16 lb and 20 lb, mainly because the basis weight of this grade is size 17 × 22. Their offset equivalents are 40 lb and 50 lb (basis weight size is 25 × 38). A smooth-finish offset paper, or regular-finish for that matter, will substitute nicely, and no one will know the difference.

If the basis weight we have sprung on you is confusing, be patient—we will explain it in due time. The days of basis weights and their resulting confusion—which we shall later explain in detail—are coming to an end. Metrication is coming to the rescue, now that the United States has passed its two hundredth birthday and is ready to join the rest of the world in a standard system of weights and measures.

Rag Bond

More important, in our opinion, is the rag bond category. The term rag is also a holdover, dating back some two centuries to the time when rags were imported from England as the only known substance from which to make paper. We gained our national independence in more ways than one when we discovered that wood fibers were plentiful in our own forests—an unparalleled substance which renews itself.

Rags are made from cotton. The fact that we can reclaim cotton which has been previously used for making men's shirts or ladies' dresses is important to our life cycle. Or, for that matter, the remnants of cotton manufacture, the cutoffs from predesigned clothing or cotton goods, have found a useful place among our speciality paper mills. Pure cotton is also used in making cotton, or rag content, papers. (See Figure 4-1.)

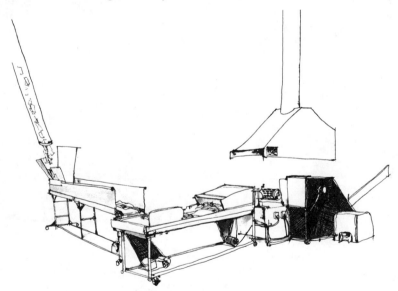

Figure 4-1. After cloth cuttings are inspected by sorters, they are carried on a conveyer to machines that chop them into segments about an inch square. They are passed under magnets to remove any hidden metal particles. (*Courtesy Strathmore Paper Co.*)

Rag bonds are probably most commonly used for business letter-heads. When a 25% rag is used, 25% of the furnish is cotton content and 75% is wood fiber. The combination gives added strength and pleasing formation. The paper manufacturing process is essentially the same as for other papers, with beating, bleaching, refining, fillers, and the like. The final finishing process is probably the major difference. The rag bonds can be made with either a smooth or a cockle finish (See Figure 4-2). Laid patterns are also quite common in this specialty paper. Universally, all these papers are watermarked to specify their cotton content.

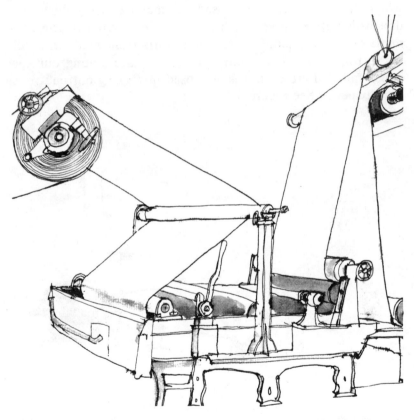

Other Rag Bonds

Bonds that are 50% rag, 75% rag, as the names imply, have that much cotton content with wood fiber accounting for the balance, while 100% rag is all cotton fiber. The watermarked paper must define the cotton content. As you can well imagine, the higher the rag content, the more expensive the sheet.

The word "white" in this case is a dangerous word. There are plain whites, fluorescent whites, cream whites, or whatever the

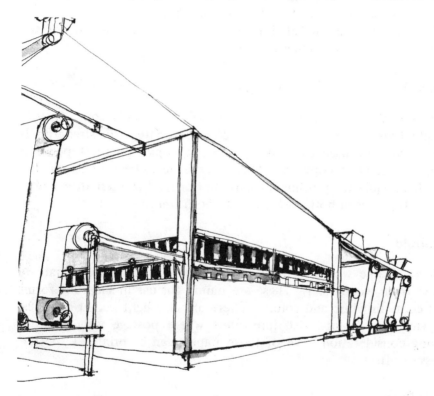

Figure 4-2. Cockle finish on rag content papers is attained by saturating the paper in a special sizing solution and then air-drying the web in a long, heated tunnel. The tension of the web, the temperature in the tunnel, and the speed of movement are carefully controlled, determining the precise amount of shrinkage and the exact degree of cockle. (*Courtesy Strathmore Paper Co.*)

manufacturer states is his shade of white. Play it safe and get mill samples before you order.

There are two more rag bonds we might mention. One is called "Ezerase," or some trade name to this effect, to signify added erasability. It is slightly more costly than the regular rag bond and is available so that the scar of erasures can be minimized, or made hard to detect. This type of rag bond is commonly used by law firms when drawing up contracts, or perhaps reporting testimony from a witness. The other type is called "Extra #1 100% Rag." The latter uses the highest-quality cotton fiber.

Continuing with uncoated papers, we have the light end of the paper scale in several grades or types.

Onion Skin

First is the well known onion skin. This generally comes in 9 lb weight (basis 17 X 22) and has a 25% rag content for strength. It was commonly used for making multiple copies on the typewriter prior to the photocopy era. This usage is declining, but onion skin is still valuable for printing air mail stationery for international mail users. It comes in both cockle and smooth finishes.

Manifold

Next in line would be the light-weight manifold papers that are made from wood fiber. These are handy for use in snap-out forms and come in white and colors. There are also light-weight opaques, in white and colors, also important where postage weights are a strong consideration. All of these papers can be printed by letter-press or offset.

Bible Paper

Another classification in light-weight paper is the thin, or bible, paper. Inasmuch as the bulk of these papers is very low, one has to consider a printing process that is suitable. While they can be printed by sheet-fed letterpress or offset, this can be done only with difficulty and at low running speeds. In addition, they would be hard to fold without creasing, and again only with careful handling and running at a slow pace.

The best answer from a printing standpoint is to use a web-fed operation. Paper in rolls goes through a web press under constant tension and at relatively high speed; also, the web permits the paper to be folded into signatures as an in-line operation, so that both of the obstacles to sheet-fed printing are overcome.

Light-weight Papers

While we have these great advantages of light weight usage, we must also be conscious of the cost from the paper mill standpoint. Light-weight papers take much longer to manufacture and therefore command a premium price. Since paper is sold by the pound rather than the yard, there are obviously more yards and fewer pounds to thin papers, and the price must be adjusted accordingly.

Bible papers are used where the consumer, or publisher, has a great number of pages to fit into a book. If the paper were, for example, 50 lb basis, the thickness of the book and the cost of binding might be prohibitive. Shipping costs, whether by postal service or truck or air transportation, might well compensate for the higher price paid for thin paper. This matter requires careful planning by the consumer before making a final decision.

Carbonless Paper

In the specialty paper category, the carbonless type has been very popular. NCR papers are probably the best known, although carbonless papers are also made by other manufacturers.

Carbonless papers have a coating that we might describe as being invisible but always present. The advantage of this paper is that no messy carbon paper is involved. The disadvantage is its sensitivity to scuffing or marring. The best way to describe its use is by illustration.

Suppose you wanted a three-part business form and decided to use a carbonless paper. Generally you would specify white as the first copy, perhaps yellow and pink for the next two copies. Assume the size to be $8\frac{1}{2} \times 11$. How would you order the paper? The fact that the paper is priced in dollars per thousand sheets is incidental to our discussion. The important specification is: white CB (coated back), yellow CFB (coated front and back), pink CF (coated front).

These papers can be printed on both sides, regardless of the coating. The coating is important for the purpose of transferring the image, by typewriter, ball point pen, or the like. The impression on the white paper passes through onto the yellow by virtue of its coated back in contact with the front coating of the yellow. In turn, the impression on the yellow is transferred by virtue of its back coating onto the pink paper because it has a coated front. In summary, carbonless papers must have the proper coatings in the proper places in order to transfer the desired image.

Carbonless papers are expensive in relation to other printing papers, but they have their redeeming features. From the printing standpoint, the papers come in varying sizes, in multiples of $8\frac{1}{2} \times 11$ or $8\frac{1}{2} \times 14$. This permits large-size forms, as well as offering the economy of printing large quantities in multiples to save money. When cutting, however, the printer or binder must be careful in handling so as not to create scuff marks, especially when clamping the paper just prior to the actual cut.

Reverse Order

Another good feature of papers like the NCR type is the ability to purchase them in "reverse order." For example, in our three-part form, the three-part set would come precollated as pink, yellow, and white. After printing, the papers would reverse themselves into the proper sequence, saving a collating operation. The paper sets can then be padded with a special padding cement and fanned apart. The three-part set would stick together, separating at the appropriate point. This is referred to as the "fan-apart" process.

It may be useful to know that besides the regular-weight carbonless bond papers, there are also coated ledger and coated tag. These are heavier-weight papers, which will stand up better in a file drawer or other filing receptacle that requires more rigidity.

Gummed papers are another specialty for addressing labels. These papers come in coated and uncoated fronts, even cast-coated, such as Kromekote. The desirable feature is to have a curl-proof paper, often with a dry back. This is important in offset printing because of the use of water in addition to ink.

Text Papers

Text papers and covers are the next category, the most expensive uncoated because of their superior grade. They come in a large variety of colors and finishes but have a somewhat limited weight basis. For example, most text papers are only available in 70 lb and 80 lb basis. The cover weights are usually 65 lb and 80 lb basis. There are many text papers that only come in 80 lb paper weight, with the corresponding color and finish only in 80 lb cover.

Text papers, because of their superior manufacturing quality, are generally used for prestige-type printing. First among those applications would be annual and periodic corporate reports. Since it is considered good taste to have the heavier cover stock match the inside, text papers are a natural choice for the discriminating buyer.

The finishes or patterns are virtually impossible to describe because of the large variety of names assigned by the various paper mills. Likewise, colors vary. Common color designations, such as ivory, blue, green, and red, are almost meaningless for selection purposes—the only way to make a selection is to have a sample swatch book or request samples from a distributor who handles that particular mill line . . . and not every paper distributor handles every mill paper line.

Text Paper Finishes

The finishes can be put on the papers in several ways. First, the dandy roll at the wet end of the machine may be used. Second, many text papers have special felt finishes that, as their name implies, are put on the paper by felts specially designed for the purpose. Third, a finish can be put on text paper off the machine by using a special embossing pattern (Figure 4-3).

Figure 4-3. Embosser. Some commercial printing papers are embossed to give them a textured surface. Paper passes between an engraved metal roll and a soft composition backing roll. The engraved design is pressed into the paper's coated surface. (*Courtesy S. D. Warren Co.*)

Many experienced people try to guess the basis weight of paper by taking the edge of a sheet between the thumb and forefinger and judging thickness in that manner. Too often one can be fooled by text papers because of the compression that has taken place in the embossing process. It might be hard to realize that an embossed text paper, feeling like a light-weight 70 lb is actually 80 lb. The same situation often occurs when an 80 lb cover feels like a 65-lb sheet. Needless to say, a micrometer will help. A mill swatch book will also be an accurate guide.

Other uses for fancy-finish text papers are in prestige promotion pieces. Some people like to be different and use fancy-finish colored papers for letterheads. Fancy endleaf papers constitute another use, in a high-quality book that is case-bound.

Cover Stock

Cover stocks also come in plain finishes without an embossing pattern. They might come in antique, vellum, or smooth finishes. In any case, cover stocks have a good-quality feel, are carefully prepared, and are priced accordingly. They have excellent affinity for ink and perform well in color printing.

Text papers and covers are good for announcements, invitations, and the like. In such cases, matching envelopes are desirable. It is always advisable to prepare promotion announcements, greeting cards, and other items in such a manner as to fit some of the envelope standards. The variety is adequate for every purpose.

Deckle Edge

A final word about text papers concerns the deckle edge. This is a fancy, wavy edge, or deckle, put on the paper by squirting a steady stream of water at an angle at the wet end of the machine. The continued use of the deckle edge is questionable, however, because of the concern for water pollution.

Coated Paper

Coated paper is our next area of interest. The quality of coated varies widely and so does the cost.

One of the largest uses of coated is in publications. The mass media use machine coated paper almost exclusively, as does the business paper field. In the first instance, coated stock is made for letterpress, lithography, and gravure. Perhaps we should ask why? Why not uncoated?

A few decades ago, before coated papers were so prominent, consumer publications used a supercalendered uncoated paper.

Letterpress was the primary printing process at that time, and the reproduction of halftones demanded a smooth sheet, hence the use of supercalendering.

Coated papers offered many more advantages, however. The clay fillers not only gave smoothness to these papers, they also added considerable opacity. The disadvantage was the high cost.

The cost factor was largely overcome by the innovation of adding a coating to the paper in an on-line papermaking operation. Thus, after the paper had passed through the drier section, it passed through a coating machine and then continued on into an after-drier operation before winding on the reel as a finished product. This process is continuous. The web of paper, coated while still in manufacture, took on the name of machine coated in contrast to a coating process that had always been done off the machine as a separate operation.

Another economy measure used by the large consumer magazines is to have a partial groundwood content as part of the furnish, perhaps 25% to 40%. Still another angle is to cut down the basis weight of the paper. The standard used to be 40 or 45 lb machine coated. The publishers demanded still more economy, so the paper dropped to 38 lb, then 36 lb, then down to 34 lb. No one dares to say that the lower limit has been reached, even though many people think it has.

This exceedingly light weight has called for much research by all parties concerned. The paper manufacturers had to maintain some strength factors as well as uniformity of roll winding. At the same time the base stock had to be uniform, as did travel on a fourdrinier machine at speeds which might exceed 3,000 feet per minute. Ink receptivity, especially when printing four-color process, was another challenge. The press manufacturers also had to do their bit by providing high-speed operation, minimum web breaks, and quick drying of the paper. A quick study of our consumer publications will confirm the fact that success has been attained.

The next higher grade of machine coated, if one can talk about grades as such, eliminates all groundwood content and uses only chemical-free paper. This sort of stock is used by business magazine publishers where the quantity of paper per issue is comparatively small, meaning a fractional part of a carload (perhaps 10,000 to 15,000 lb). In such cases the basis weight might be anywhere from 45 to 60 lb and it would probably be whiter in color than the consumer magazine stock.

The better grades of coated paper are whiter in color and go through several layers of coating in order to obtain a smoother surface when better grades are required. The paper consists of a base stock, to which is added one or more layers of mineral pigments bonded with adhesives. For strength, the stock favors a softwood fiber because of its length, combined with short-fiber hardwoods for filler. This is an ideal combination, giving both strength and smoothness to the body stock in preparation for the coating. After the coating operation is complete, the paper is then supercalendered for added smoothness.

Coated Paper Use

At this point, we should reflect on the use of coated paper and on when it can best be used. First, coated papers offer the advantage of greater smoothness than uncoated, providing an ideal situation for printing halftones by all processes, particularly in the case of process color. If more brilliance is desired, the whiter the sheet, the better will be the reflectivity of the inks and the sharper the contrast. Of course, the proper pigments should be added, particularly titanium dioxide for greater whiteness.

Opacity is better in coated stock because of the pigmented coatings, as well as the smooth paper formation.

One of the greatest disadvantages of coated paper is its low bulk for its basis weight. The paper is also somewhat limp, in contrast to uncoated paper, which is bulkier and more rigid.

Annual reports and quality printing of halftones are well suited uses for coated stock. In addition to the book, or text, weights, coated papers also come in cover weights, offering the advantage of a matching set of text and cover coated.

Dull Coated

Another possibility is dull coated papers. As an alternative to a high-gloss finish that might be bothersome to people who like the quality of coated but not the shine, dull coated was created. Many textbooks have utilized this nonglare effect to good advantage. Everyone has different taste: some prefer gloss coated, others prefer the nonglare papers. It is important to emphasize that all of the desirable qualities of coated paper are retained in dull coated. Some of these characteristics are ink holdout, ink receptivity, high opacity, and a top-notch printing surface.

Cast Coated

The ultimate in coated papers is the cast coated type. These papers are made by pressing the wet coated surface of the paper against a heated and highly polished chrome-plated dryer. When dry, the sheet has a bright, mirrorlike surface and is very smooth. Many of these papers come cast coated on one side only. If the same coating is to be placed on both sides, the process has to be repeated for the opposite side. The manufacturing process is slow, and the cost is high—about double the cost of enamel papers. These cast coated papers come in both text and cover weights.

Litho Coated

Another type of coated paper is litho coated one side. As the name indicates, there is coating on one side of the paper only. It is most often used for industrial wrapping, for mounting a sheet to board, or as book jackets. In cost, it is about equal to the regular coated-two-side paper.

The final variation of coated is matte finish paper, which might be described as a dull coated with a toothy finish. In the dull coated papers, there is less polishing in the calender stack, since a dull finish is desired. In the matte finish, the paper would take only a light nip to smooth down the paper as a final step before rewinding. Obviously this would give a slightly greater bulk to the matte coated papers.

Bristol, Index, Tag

Another category in the important list of everyday papers is bristol. It can be augmented by almost similar papers such as index and tag.

In the economy class, there is vellum bristol, which is very bulky for its basis weight and deliberately designed that way. One of the greatest uses for such papers used to be for business reply cards. When postal requirements called for 9 points of bulk (.009 inch), a 67 lb basis vellum bristol was made to fill the need. When the postal service dropped the minimum bulk requirements, the paper mills obliged with a 57 lb vellum bristol for the same reason. Since the postal bulk requirements have tentatively dropped to 6 points (.006 inch), a vellum finish 70 lb offset sheet should meet that requirement.

The next category of bristol is often referred to as "printing bristol." This is a bad description because in most cases bristol is ordered with the intent to print on it. Some people refer to it as "mill bristol," a better designation because it takes away the inference that a cheaper grade, such as the high-bulk vellum bristols, may not be printable, which, of course, is not so.

This bristol is more condensed than the vellum bristol, giving it better feel and also providing a better printing surface for quality printing. Some of these bristols are also coated, on one or two sides as required. This type of quality bristol is ideal for soft-cover books (as distinguished from the case-bound type) as well as being used for all sorts of advertising and public relations literature.

Index bristol is commonly used for index cards. Here, again, the difference is a fine one from the mill bristol counterpart. Some people may say that the mill bristol is formed on a cylinder machine and that the index is produced by the fourdrinier process. Tomorrow these papers may also be produced on a twin wire machine—

who can tell? The differences can better be understood by understanding the basic process of manufacture, as well as the content of
the furnish. In other words, how much softwood and/or hardwood
content is there? How heavily have the fibers been beaten to form a
better and closer mesh? How much, and what type, of fillers have
been used?

If die cutting is one of the finishing processes, a strong, sturdy
sheet is most desirable. For folding purposes, scoring is a must in
heavier-weight papers.

Next we speak of tag. Strength is the most important characteristic here, and the fiber formation is not as well-meshed as in bristols.
Obviously a kraft manufacturing process is used for this purpose.

File folders may well represent the best-known use of tag papers.
They have to be strong for durability and wear. The paper, like
other bristols, is made in various colors. Tag can also be coated,
if desired.

It is our belief that the terminology of the bristols, tags, and index
is somewhat misleading because of the changes in manufacturing that
are taking place. In other words, the papers are getting too close to
one another in characteristics. Since we must be aware of present
conditions as well as future possibilities, we have to cover every
aspect of the picture.

There is still another type of bristol, used for business cards, announcements, and the like where top quality is desired. The fibers
are well beaten, high-quality fillers are used, and the formation
is excellent. Obviously the price is much higher than that of the mill
bristol—approximately 50% higher. These papers come in smooth
and vellum finishes. Of course, they do add to the confusion of
paper definition, unfortunately. Even worse, some of these fine, or
rather *superfine*, bristols have some rag content, which adds more
strength—and higher costs.

We don't mean to be sarcastic about the fine points of these various papers, but we'll pull no punches in saying that there is much
confusion for the novice in trying to understand all of the differences
in papers that are so close to each other in manufacture. This is

especially emphasizes when we come to the discussion of basis weights.

Be patient—there is much hope for change, and that change is already on the horizon, as we shall discuss later.

5
PAPER—
HOW TO BUY IT

In order to know how to buy paper, it is important to understand the basis weights of the various grades, as well as the sizes that can be bought. Also important is an understanding of carton and skid packing, since it has a direct bearing on cost.

The present method of purchasing paper is on a cost-per-pound basis, so we shall fully explore this method. At the same time we are well aware that we are in the initial stages of a transfer to the metric system, which will be covered later.

Basis Weight

First, what is basis weight? The most common weight basis is called the text weight, as distinguished from the cover weight. For example:

$$25 \times 38 = 70$$

means that 1 ream (500 sheets) of text weight paper, size 25″ × 38″ will weigh 70 lb.

Please note that we are only talking about *weight*, not color, bulk, finish, or other characteristics. In terms of *cost*, the weight of the paper multiplied by the cost per pound will give you the total purchase price. For example:

1,000 sheets of 25 × 38, basis 70 = 140 lb

This might be written by a paper merchant as:

1,000 sheets of 25 × 38 = 140

Even simpler:

1,000 sheets of 25 × 38—140M

The last item is the most common method of expression. If the price per pound is 42¢ the total cost will be:

140 × .42 = $58.80

From a practical standpoint, there are many other sizes that are used.   These will have *different M* weights although representing the same *basis* weight.

In the foregoing examples we have talked about 70 lb stock as the basis weight. Actually, there are many other weights and sizes. Also, it is mathematically easier to quote and calculate paper weights on a weight-per-thousand-sheets basis. Although the basis weight of a given paper is calculated on a ream-per-25 × 38 basis, many other sizes are used.

One common size of paper is 23 × 29, designed to fit a press of that size. Now we shall consider 60 lb stock and buy 7,200 sheets. The paper merchant's bill would look like this:

7,200 sheets, 23 × 29—84M = 605 lb

How did we arrive at this figure? Multiply 84 by 7.2 thousand and the result is 604.8 lb. As per trade custom, the amount is rounded out to the nearest whole number. We took the number 7,200 only because it represented the quantity in four even cartons.

Figuring M Weights

How did we know that 1,000 sheets of 23 × 29 stock, basis 60 lb, weighs 84 lb? A simple answer is that we looked up the figure in a a paper merchant's catalog. That's fine, because we picked a standard size. Regardless of size, here is a formula that will work under all conditions:

$$\frac{\text{Weight desired}}{\text{Basis weight}} = \frac{\text{Size desired}}{\text{Basic size}}$$

The weight desired is what we are trying to find; let's call it x. Further, we know that the basis weight is 60 lb, the size desired is 23 × 29, and the basic size is 25 × 38, by definition.

Substituting the known values in the above equation, we have:

$$\frac{x}{60} = \frac{23 \times 29}{25 \times 38}$$

Algebraically:

$$x = \frac{(23 \times 29)(60)}{25 \times 38}$$

$$x = \frac{667 \times 60}{950} = \frac{40,020}{950}$$

$$x = 42.1 \text{ or } 42 \text{ (rounded to whole number)}$$

Since the ream weight is 42, and two reams constitute 1,000 sheets, the *M weight* is 84.

Using the above formula, or equation, any size paper can be computed. By way of additional explanation, please note that we are computing square inches of a *desired* size and equating it with square inches of the *basic* size.

Another factor of importance is that most often the paper merchant computes, or quotes, cost in terms of dollars and cents per hundred pounds. This is exactly the same as cost per pound; for example, $58.35 per cwt. or $.5835 per lb.

Let's try another weight problem—a sheet size of 35 × 45 with a 50 lb basis weight. Referring to our basic formula, we let x equal the desired weight, the basis weight is 50 lb, the desired size is 35 × 45, and the basic size is 25 × 38.

Substituting the values:

$$\frac{x}{50} = \frac{35 \times 45}{25 \times 38}$$

$$x = \frac{(35 \times 45)(50)}{25 \times 38}$$

$$x = \frac{1575 \times 50}{950} = \frac{78,750}{950}$$

$$x = 82.89 \text{ or } 83 \text{ lb per ream}$$

Multiplying by 2, we now state that the weight per thousand sheets is 166. Stated more concisely:

$$35 \times 45 - 166M$$

Calculating Paper Needs for a Job

Now we'll take another example, which will really make you work rather than give you standard sizes that can easily be found in a mill swatch book or a merchant's catalog. Since this is the age of economical hand-held calculators, the arithmetic should not bother you.

Problem: A 70-lb coated sheet is to be used for making up 2,000,000 promotion pieces, printed two colors on both sides of the sheet. The sheet size is 7 × $8\frac{1}{2}$, and it is to be folded once as an envelope stuffer. The decision has been made to print the job in multiples on a two-color 43″ × 69″ press. What is the paper cost at $33.50 per cwt.?

Discussion: This is a practical problem, even though it may seem difficult to the reader, who may be confused as to where to start its solution. We have the unit cost of the paper, but we do not know how much paper is needed. Before that can be determined, we must figure out the sheet size. Let us start the easiest way by assuming a sheet size of 43 X 69 for calculating purposes, since this would give us the most number of units and minimize the press run.

Solution:

$$
\begin{array}{ll}
43 \times 69 & \text{(paper size)} \\
\underline{\ 7 \times \ 8\tfrac{1}{2}} & \text{(unit size)} \\
\ 6 \times \ 8 & \text{(48 units out)}
\end{array}
$$

Note that we divided 43 by 7 to get 6 out. Dividing 69 by $8\tfrac{1}{2}$, we get 8 out. Then, 6 X 8 = 48 units out of a sheet. Although we have one inch left over on each dimension, this amount cannot really be called wasteful, since we need gripper space and trim area. (See Figure 5-1.)

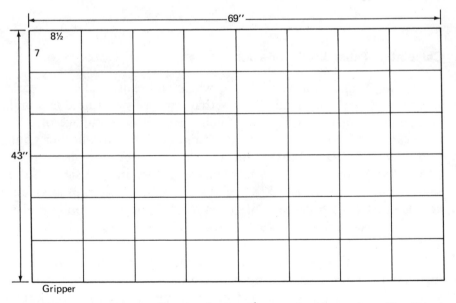

Figure 5-1. Diagram showing 48 units of a 7 X $8\tfrac{1}{2}$ promotion piece, using a 43 X 69-inch sheet. In plate-making, this would be done by using a step-and-repeat machine.

Now that we have determined the sheet size, the questions remaining are: (1) How many sheets will be needed? (2) What is the M weight of the paper? (3) What is the total cost of the paper?

Since we require 2,000,000 units and we will print 48 up, it is a simple matter to let the hand calculator do the work. (If you don't have a calculator, you can always use arithmetic). The answer comes out to 41,667 sheets. To this figure should be added a spoilage allowance; I would round it out to 43,000 sheets. It may sound inadequate to some people to place spoilage at 3.2%, but let it remain that way as being reasonably realistic.

Now we must solve the second question, the M weight. Go back to the basic formula and substitute the respective figures, as follows, with x equal to the weight desired, as usual:

$$\frac{x}{70} = \frac{43 \times 69}{25 \times 38}$$

$$x = \frac{(43 \times 69)(70)}{25 \times 38}$$

$$x = \frac{207,690}{950}$$

$$x = 219 \text{ lb per ream}$$

$$x = 438 \text{ lb per thousand sheets}$$

Restated: 43 × 69—438M.

For the benefit of those who are not too quick at arithmetic, we shall break down the component parts and then conclude the problem.

There are 43,000 sheets to be used, with an M weight of 438 lb per thousand sheets, at a cost of $33.50 per hundred pounds. Using the calculator, it may be better to use the cost per pound to avoid decimal-point problems. Therefore, we shall use $.335 per lb. The equation now reads:

Total cost = 43 × 438 × .335 = $6309.39

Note that for calculating costs we have dropped the three zeros after the 43, since 438 represents the weight of 1,000 sheets. If this is not clear, please turn back a few pages and start the problem over—it might be less confusing the second time.

Before continuing, let us do a little logical planning. The key to the above problem was to figure out the M weight of a 43 X 69 sheet. A quick estimate is that this sheet is slightly less than a 45 X 70 size (double 35 X 45). If the M weight of a 35 X 45 sheet is 232 (basis 70), then for the double size it would be 464. Actually our value turned out to be 438, which is somewhat less than 464. That means that we had to be on the right track. We assume that you would have looked into a merchant's catalog to find the M weight of the standard 35 X 45 sheet. The paper merchant's catalog offers a tremendous amount of information that is vital to paper purchasing.

Before going further, please refer to Table 5-1, which shows the type of paper, finish, basis weight, and weight per thousand sheets. In this instance the weights and substance shown are based on the text weight of 25 X 38. By definition, the substance, or basis weight, is defined as the weight per ream (500 sheets). Since it is much easier to work with decimals rather than fractions, weights are shown on a thousand-sheet basis. In parenthesis, next to the M weights, we have shown the carton packing.

Table 5-1. Illustration of a typical paper listing showing basis weight, M weight, and carton packing for a text weight sheet (basis 25 X 38).

	BASIC OFFSET Smooth and Vellum Finish WHITE		
Substance →	50	60	70
$17\frac{1}{2}$ X $22\frac{1}{2}$	41 (3600)	50 (3200)	58 (2400)
23 X 29	70 (2000)	84 (1800)	98 (1500)
23 X 35	85 (1800)	102 (1500)	119 (1200)
25 X 38	100 (1600)	120 (1200)	140 (1000)
35 X 45	166 (900)	198 (800)	232 (600)

For example, what is the M weight and carton packing of 70 lb stock, size 23 X 29? Select the paper size on the left column, move horizontally across to the column under the number 70, and the answer is 98 lb per thousand sheets, with 1,500 sheets in a carton.

Also note that the larger the sheet size, the less paper there is in each carton. Similarly, the heavier the weight, the fewer sheets there are in each carton. From these figures, we can take a rule of thumb and say that each carton of paper contains approximately 150 lb. This is a good rule to remember when a quick estimate is made of paper costs.

Paper Jobber Price Structure

Regarding cost, note the price structure in Table 5-2. The greater the quantity is, the lower the price bracket. This can be explained in terms of cost of handling and trucking. While these figures are taken from a merchant's catalog, please regard the figures as approximate only, in terms of today's prices. The drop in prices in each bracket will indicate the approximate saving as the quantities increase.

There are several interesting features about this price structure. First, note that the cost of 50 lb paper is a little higher than the 60 and 70 lb. Can you understand why? Also note that the cost of less than one carton increases by roughly 50%. Can you understand the reasoning behind this? Finally, there is a notation that states that for skid packing, deduct $1.00 per cwt, or $.01 per lb.

Table 5-2. Price structure of paper shown in Table 5-1. Note that figures are shown as cost per pound, to four decimal places, for quick calculation.

	Cost per pound						
	Less than carton	1 carton 1 item	4 cartons assorted	16 cartons assorted	5M lb 1 item	10M lb 1 item	C/L 1 item
Sub. 50	.7870	.5370	.4745	.4425	.3675	.3470	.3150
Sub. 60 & 70	.7785	.5285	.4670	.4355	.3615	.3415	.3100
					Skid allowance 1.00 cwt.		

Answering the first question, refer back to the papermaking operation. After all "makeready" operations are complete, the paper will be formed on either a fourdrinier or a twin wire machine. The speed of the wire (either one) will be at a given rate, but less furnish will be released for the lighter-weight paper. This means that it will take *longer* to produce a carload of paper (a minimum carload is defined as 36,000 lb). Likewise, if 40-lb paper is ordered, the unit price will still be higher. In the trade, this is referred to as "penalty for light weight."

Answering the second question, there is considerably more handling in shipping less than carton quantities. The carton must be broken open, the required fraction is repacked, and the remainder is put back on the shelf. The shipping, or truck delivery, costs the same as for a full carton. For planning purposes, assume that less than a carton means half a carton. If your needs are for three-fourths of a carton, it will pay you to buy the full carton and hold the balance for some possible small future requirement. If the order calls for much less than half a carton, the paper house will assess its minimum order charge.

The third item is the skid packing allowance. This would refer to the larger paper quantities. A normal skid packing is approximately 3,000 lb. If 5,000 lb were ordered, it might well be packed in two even skids. Once again, it is quicker to pack paper on a skid rather than to package separate cartons.

Going back to our rule of thumb, we said that a carton of any size paper will weigh about 150 lb. Four cartons will then weigh approximately 600 lb (sometimes referred to as a "case"), while 16 cartons will weigh approximately a ton. The other price brackets are self-explanatory. The minimum carload is 36,000 lb, although the same freight car will easily hold at least twice as much.

Cover Stock

The next category of paper is cover stock. Most covers come in two basis weights, 65 and 80 lb. However, the basic size, or basis weight size, is 20 X 26. By definition, one ream of cover stock, size

20 × 26, will weigh 65 or 80 lb. Once again we have changed the basis for calculation. This is further complicated by the fact that there is such an item as 80 lb text weight basis, as well as 80 lb cover. The weights of the two are considerably different.

For example, using our formula to determine the weight of a given size paper, let us calculate the weight of 23 × 35 cover stock, basis 80.

Let x equal the desired weight of cover stock. The same formula, regardless of stock, will work:

$$\frac{\text{Weight desired}}{\text{Basis weight}} = \frac{\text{Size desired}}{\text{Basic size}}$$

$$\frac{x}{80} = \frac{23 \times 35}{20 \times 26}$$

$$x = \frac{(23 \times 35)(80)}{20 \times 26}$$

$$x = \frac{805 \times 80}{520} = \frac{64,400}{520}$$

$$x = 124 \text{ lb per ream}$$

$$x = 248 \text{ lb per thousand sheets}$$

in other words, 23 × 35–248M.

Substituting in the same formula for 80 lb text weight:

$$\frac{x}{80} = \frac{23 \times 35}{25 \times 38}$$

$$x = \frac{(23 \times 35)(80)}{950}$$

$$x = \frac{64,400}{950}$$

$$x = 68 \text{ lb per ream}$$

$$x = 136 \text{ lb per thousand sheets}$$

Once again, we have 23 X 35—136M.

Note the considerable difference in M weights between the text and cover weights. When spelled out arithmetically, the difference is clear. However, when ordering paper, be sure to *emphasize* either text or cover weight basis.

Regarding price structure and packing, refer to Table 5-3.

Table 5-3. Listing of the three most common cover weight sizes, with their corresponding M weights and carton packing.

Substance →	WHITE 65	80
20 X 26	130 (1000)	160 (750)
23 X 35	201 (750)	248 (500)
26 X 40	260 (500)	320 (500)

Cover Price Variations

Fancy-finish cover stocks can vary greatly in price, from one mill to another, from one color or pattern to another. Also, some very special stocks will come only in one size and weight. For example, a deep red might be available only in 80 lb text and 80 lb cover with only one cover size—26 X 40. Generally speaking, the mills will match the text weight and finish with a cover stock with the same pattern. Sizes, however, may be limited to only one or two.

Regarding price structure, you can assume that the colors will cost more than white. Let your assumption stop at that point because different colors *may* command different prices. For exact costs, consult your paper merchant. Perhaps his price list will be up to date, but don't count on it. Prices have a habit of changing faster than the merchant can print them.

In Table 5-4 there is a price list differential, with the names deliberately changed. Note the surprising number of variations in costs and descriptions.

Table 5-4. Varying prices of a fancy-finish cover stock, with costs differing for both colors and finish.

	Unit 1 Item	1 Carton	4 Cartons	16 Cartons	5000 lb
SUPERB COVER Price per pound					
Smooth Finish					
Blue or Cream White	.7965	.6465	.5705	.5320	.4385
Ivory	.8175	.6675	.5895	.5500	.4535
Regular colors	.8305	.6805	.6010	.5605	.4625
Gold or Purple	.8480	.6980	.6160	.5745	.4745
Dark Blue, Dark Green, Bright Orange	.8650	.7150	.6310	.5885	.4870
Star Gold, Star Green, Star Yellow	.8820	.7320	.6465	.6030	.4990
Black	.9165	.7665	.6765	.6310	.5230
Red	.9335	.7835	.6920	.6455	.5355
Feldspar Finish					
Azure White	—	.6935	.6125	.5710	.4625
Ivory	—	.7150	.6310	.5885	.4775
Gray	—	.7280	.6425	.5995	.4870
Gold or Purple	—	.7450	.6575	.6135	.4990
Dark Green, Orange	—	.7620	.6730	.6275	.5110
Star Gold, Star Green, Star Yellow	—	.7795	.6880	.6420	.5230

While on the subject of text papers, you should be aware of the fact that these fancy grades are almost always available in envelopes. If the paper merchant does not have a particular envelope in stock, he will give you an availability date when converters are having a run on them. If your order is large enough, you may want to convert text papers yourself with an envelope house which specializes in this field. They will have both the dies and the equipment for converting, in most cases.

Grain Direction

One of the problems frequently encountered with cover stock is grain direction. Too often a printing job favors grain long and then

becomes grain short for folding. This difficulty may be partly overcome by scoring the cover and then folding on the score. Coated
covers, especially the cast coated type, have a tendency to crack even
with a score.

Continuing further with grain direction problems, it is always good
to know what alternatives are available. Let us assume that you are
faced with a short press run on cover stock and need a size 26 × 20.
The standard size of 20 × 26 means that the grain is in the 26 inch
direction. Customarily, we list the width as the first dimension and
the depth as the second size. For emphasis, or to clarify further the
grain direction, an underline is used so that there is no doubt that
26 × 20 means grain 20.

Sometimes there are stocks made with the grain both ways, but not
usually. The solution to the above problem is to get a double-size
sheet, or 26 × 40. This is a mill standard and can be cut in half to
meet grain requirements.

Another common cover stock size is 23 × 35. The grain is in the
35″ dimension but you may need the grain the 23″ way. A solution
may be cover stocks that are made in size 35 × 46. Once again, cut
the stock in half to meet the requirement.

To round out the cover stock picture, some covers are also available in 23 × 29 size, though not too many.

Figuring Cover Stock Needs

One of the problems that arise frequently is to obtain a cover stock
that will accommodate an $8\frac{1}{2}$ × 11 bleed size. If the cover is for a
publication or booklet or catalog, you must add the trim fractions of
approximately $\frac{1}{4}''$ in each direction. With the bleed factor, you need
a minimum of $17\frac{1}{2}$ × $11\frac{1}{2}$. Add to this the gripper margin, and possibly a spine to cover the thickness, and you immediately think you
have plenty of room with a 19 × 25 sheet. Unfortunately cover
stocks only come 20 × 26, so you have to accept the additional
waste.

On second thought, perhaps we are passing over too quickly the
publication cover we have mentioned above. In that case, study the
diagrams in Figure 5-2.

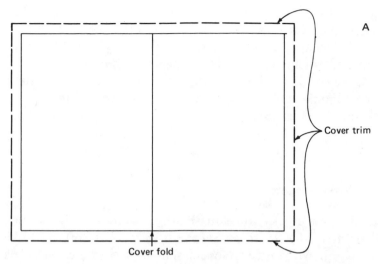

A

Cover trim

Cover fold

Figure 5-2. (A) Cover for a saddle-stitch publication where the fold is in the center. The entire book is trimmed on top, bottom, and outside after stitching. (B) Cover for a "side gathered" book, either adhesive or Smyth, with an allowance of stock for the spine. After gathering and adhering of the cover, the entire book is trimmed in the same manner as above.

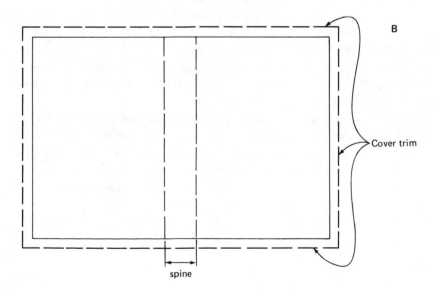

B

Cover trim

spine

Figure 5-2A depicts a saddle-stitch type of binding where the cover fold is in the center of the sheet. When the cover and the insides have been collated, a guillotine cut of at least $\frac{1}{8}''$ is made on the top, bottom, and outside to open up the pages of the book.

In Figure 5-2B, the book contains too many pages for the saddle type of binding and would be either adhesive (perfect) bound or Smyth sewn. Thus an appropriate space is left at the spine to wrap the cover around the book comfortably. The two folds at the spine would be scored to make a better binding job.

Coated Cover Weights

Coated cover stocks come in slightly different weights, although based on the 20 X 26 size. Standard weights are 60 lb, 80 lb, and 100 lb cover, with price brackets similar to those of other papers. Many mills also feature an embossed coated, which adds a special pattern or finish to the coated sheet.

The cast coated papers, those with a high-lustre finish, have a different pricing structure. The text papers, such as 80 lb and 100 lb basis, come in the standard sizes with regular pricing. The cover stocks, however, are designated differently.

In cast coated cover, the paper comes both coated one side (C1S) and coated two sides (C2S). The description, or designation, is more sensible, being quoted in point thickness: e.g., 6 pt., 8 pt., 10 pt., and so on. For easier understanding, these can be rewritten as .006″, .008″, or .010″, expressed as 6, 8, or 10 thousandths of an inch. There are additional thicknesses available.

In Table 5-5 we have made a chart of 6, 8, and 10 pt. stock, both coated one side and coated two sides. The carton packing is the same for corresponding sizes and thicknesses, but there is a slight variation in weights. For example, notice the 20 X 26 size in 6 pt. stock. The C1S weighs 128 lb per thousand sheets, while the C2S weighs 126 lb. The carton packing is 1,200 sheets in both cases. Thus the formulation of base stock and coating must be different in each case. In a few cases the weight per thousand sheets coincides; e.g., in the 23 X 35 size.

Table 5-5. Chart showing weight and carton packing of cast coated cover stock, both coated one side and coated two sides.

	6 Pt.	8 Pt.	10 Pt.
Cast Coated C1S			
20 × 26	128 (1200)	154 (1000)	178 (800)
23 × 29	164 (900)	198 (700)	228 (600)
23 × 35	198 (700)	238 (600)	275 (500)
26 × 40	256 (600)	308 (500)	356 (400)
35 × 46	396 (400)	476 (300)	550 (250)
Cast Coated C2S			
20 × 26	126 (1200)	153 (1000)	177 (800)
23 × 29	162 (900)	197 (700)	228 (600)
23 × 35	195 (700)	237 (600)	275 (500)
26 × 40	252 (600)	306 (500)	354 (400)
35 × 46	390 (400)	474 (300)	550 (250)

The price structure of cast coated is different, in that the cost is listed per 1,000 sheets. In Table 5-6 we have shown a listing of the costs of C2S and a partial listing of C1S. As with all papers, the cost decreases as the quantity increases. Also note the comparison of costs between C1S and C2S. It is also interesting to note the allowance of skid packing vs. carton packing. As we have mentioned before, the normal skid weight is approximately 3,000 lb.

Bond Papers

The next category of paper would be in the "business papers" area, the most common of which is known as bond. The bonds are either rag content or non–rag content. The non–rag content is known as sulfite bond. Both types have one thing in common—the basic size is 17 × 22.

Business offices use 16 and 20-lb bond for general office use. By definition, one ream of bond paper, size 17″ × 22″ weighs either 16 or 20 lb. Listing it on a per-thousand-sheets basis, weights would be restated as:

Table 5-6. Listing of cast coated C2S and partial listing of cast coated C1S showing comparison of prices, both cartons and skids.

	Per 1000 sheets				
	1 carton 1 item	4 cartons assorted	16 cartons assorted	5M lb 1 item	10M lb 1 item
Cast Coated Cover C2S					
8 Point White					
20 × 26 cartons	121.35	106.55	97.90	83.75	81.25
skids				82.45	79.95
23 × 29 cartons	155.60	136.95	125.50	107.50	104.25
skids				105.80	102.55
23 × 35 cartons	187.80	164.90	151.50	129.75	125.80
skids				127.35	123.80
26 × 40 cartons	242.65	213.05	195.75	167.65	162.65
skids				165.05	159.95
35 × 46 cartons	375.65	329.80	303.00	259.50	251.60
skids				255.45	247.55
Cast Coated Cover C1S					
8 Point White					
20 × 26 cartons	100.15	88.00	80.70	69.00	65.05
skids				67.70	63.75
23 × 29 cartons	128.40	112.80	103.45	88.45	83.45
skids				86.80	81.75
23 × 35 cartons	155.00	136.20	124.90	106.75	100.65
skids				104.75	98.65

$$17 \times 22 - 32M$$

$$17 \times 22 - 40M$$

Like other printing papers, these bonds also come in multiple sizes, both for press economy and for the ability to get the paper grain in a desired direction. For example, if you wanted to purchase a 22 × 17 sheet, with the grain in the 17″ direction, you would have to purchase a 22 × 34 size and cut the paper in half.

For the last time in this chapter we tackle the problem of converting to a size when all that is known is the basis weight. This formula will work for any type of paper.

Problem: What is the M weight (weight per thousand sheets) of a bond size 28 × 34, substance 20?

Solution:

$$\frac{\text{Desired weight}}{\text{Basis weight}} = \frac{\text{Desired size}}{\text{Basic size}}$$

$$\frac{x}{20} = \frac{28 \times 34}{17 \times 22}$$

$$x = \frac{(28 \times 34)(20)}{17 \times 22}$$

$$x = \frac{19,040}{374}$$

$$x = 51 \text{ lb per ream}$$

$$x = 102 \text{ lb per M}$$

Restated: 28 × 34 −102M.

Once again, we might study the weight, size, and carton packing of bond papers to get acquainted with this important paper category. Refer to Table 5-7.

Table 5-7. Listing of basic sizes, weights, and carton packing (items in parenthesis) of sulfite bond papers. These sizes are not necessarily available in every mill brand.

| | SULFITE BOND | | |
Substance →	16	20	24
17 × 22	32 (4000)	40 (3000)	48 (3000)
17½ × 22½	34 (4000)	42 (3000)	
17 × 28	41 (3000)	51 (3000)	61 (2000)
19 × 24	39 (3000)	49 (3000)	59 (2000)
22 × 34	64 (2000)	80 (1500)	96 (1500)
38 × 24	78 (1500)	98 (1500)	
34 × 28	82 (1500)	102 (1500)	

Although 16 and 20 lb bonds are the most common, sometimes it is desirable to get a slightly heavier weight. As with other papers, also note that in the last weight bracket not every size is available. Also note the additional size of $17\frac{1}{2} \times 22\frac{1}{2}$. The extra fraction is often important in using "bleeds."

Colored Bond

Bond papers also come in colors, with every mill having different shades. Once again, refer to a mill swatch book for the colors you desire, or ask your paper merchant for samples of the papers you contemplate using. Most large paper merchants maintain a sample department to take care of such requests. Regarding paper sizes in colors, they are limited to the most often used sizes and weights.

We will dispense with the price chart for the above but offer a brief explanation. First, 16 lb bond is $1\frac{1}{2} ¢$ more in cost than 20 lb bond. By this time you are probably aware of the reason—an upcharge for light weight. In colors, the same rule applies regarding weights. Of course, colored papers command a higher price than their white counterparts because of the added chemicals and dyes.

Sulfite bonds also come in No. 1 and No. 4 grades, with a No. 5 grade sometimes available. The No. 1 grade is usually watermarked with the brand name. Speaking of watermarks, there are also linen and laid patterns available in many bond papers. As for the terminology "white," be careful—there are too many shades of white. Get samples and play it safe.

Rag Bond

Now we come to the rag bonds—25%, 50%, 75%, 100%, and a super 100% known as "Extra #1." As we have discussed before, "25% rag" means 25% cotton fiber and the balance wood fiber. The cotton fiber need not be freshly plucked from the cotton fields—fabrics that are made of cotton only (not synthetics) often have waste cuttings in manufacturing, and these are reclaimed by the rag bond paper manufacturers. In like manner, if the cuttings in question are colored, the dyes are bleached out in the paper manufacturing process and utilized. (See Figure 5-3.)

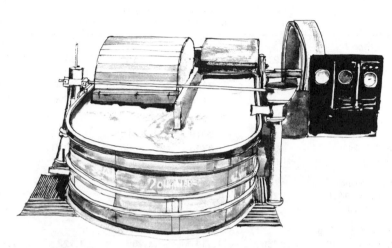

Figure 5-3. After cooking, the cotton cuttings are washed and further broken down to the fiber size appropriate for papermaking. This is done in large oval tubs, where they are circulated in a continuous flow of clean water while being abraded. Bleach is added to whiten the fibers. (*Courtesy Strathmore Paper Co.*)

Once again, not every size is available on every manufacturer's grade, but there are sizes that are a multiple of $8\frac{1}{2} \times 11$ and $8\frac{1}{2} \times 14$ in most cases. The bonds come in white and colors, with several shades of white, in cockle and laid finishes if desired. Basis weights are 13 lb, 16 lb, 20 lb, and 24 lb.

Large users of rag bond papers often like to have their own company logos watermarked in the stationery. This is done by purchasing a special die that is placed on the dandy roll at the time of manufacture. Needless to say, there must be a sizable tonnage ordered to justify this special procedure. The die purchase is made by the customer and held by the paper mill for future use.

In Table 5-8 we have constructed a pricing chart to give you an approximate idea of costs. These are arbitrary figures and will probably be much higher when you are in the market to make a purchase.

Table 5-8. Cost per pound of the various rag bond contents. Note the upcharge in light-weight papers, those under 20 lb.

	1 carton 1 item	4 cartons assorted	16 cartons assorted	5M lb assorted	10M lb assorted
25% Rag Bond					
White sub 13, 16	.9150	.8155	.7545	.6600	.6290
sub 20, 24	.8815	.7855	.7265	.6355	.6055
Colors sub 16	.9480	.8450	.7815	.6840	.6815
sub 20	.9150	.8155	.7545	.6600	.6290
50% Rag Bond					
White sub 13, 16	1.011	.9010	.8330	.7290	.6950
sub 20, 24	.9780	.8715	.8060	.7050	.6720
Colors sub 20	1.011	.9010	.8330	.7290	.6950
100% Rag Bond					
White sub 13, 16	1.395	1.251	1.178	1.052	1.007
sub 20, 24	1.363	1.222	1.152	1.028	.9835
Extra #1, 100% Rag					
White sub 13, 16	1.486	1.334	1.256	1.122	1.073
sub 20, 24, 28	1.455	1.305	1.230	1.098	1.050

Since the sizes and weights are approximately equal to the figures shown for sulfite bonds, we shall only list the price structure.

Once again you will note the upcharge for light-weight papers. The same applies to colored stock. Also note the additional costs of Extra #1 100% rag bond.

Cut Sizes

A popular feature of bond papers, as well as onion skin, is cut sizes. The most popular is $8\frac{1}{2} \times 11$, in both 16 and 20 lb bond, sulfite and rag varieties. Also available is $8\frac{1}{2} \times 14$, commonly known as legal size. These papers are quoted on a per-thousand-sheet basis, with 5,000 sheets in a carton. Onion skin comes in both smooth and cockle finishes and is always light-weight, generally 9 lb basis. It is also used for air mail stationery where foreign rates are quoted per half ounce.

Other business papers are manifold, mimeo, and duplicator, to complete the group. All of the business papers have a basic size of 17 X 22, the basis on which weight categories are quoted.

The last major category of printing papers includes bristol, index, and tag. Although, generally speaking, the three are closely related in characteristics, ironically all three have different basic sizes!

Tag, Index

Let us consider tag, a strong sheet, economical and widely used in industrial packaging. White is the most widely used color, although manila tag is commonly used for file folders. Colored tag is also available in the usual common variety of basic colors. The basic size is 24 X 36. The weights range from 100 to 200 lb.

The next item is index, a good sheet that is used for the common 3 X 5 or 4 X 6 index cards. It can be employed for any promotional use where a good stiff sheet with good snap is desired. The basic size is now $25\frac{1}{2}$ X $30\frac{1}{2}$, and the weights range from 90 to 110 to 140 lb. This variety is undoubtedly confusing to most people, but we shall try to shed some more light on the subject before the end of this book.

Not too long ago the basic size of index was $20\frac{1}{4}$ X $24\frac{3}{4}$. At that time, the three basic weights were 59, 72, and 91 lb. When we refer to the three sets of basic weights, namely 90, 110, and 140, we are indulging in semantics, since they are exactly equivalent to the old set in every way. To the novice we can only apologize for the confusion, but take heed—the metric system, which is just surfacing in the United States, will make the subject less confusing.

In our humble opinion, the day should come when both of the above-mentioned stocks merge into one grade. With respect to cost, see how they are priced in Table 5-9. The light-weight stocks in each case have a slight upward charge. Otherwise, the costs of both grades show very little differential.

Some index stocks also have a rag content, from 25% to as much as 100%, which gives great strength and quality. The cost reflects the additional cotton fiber content.

Table 5-9. Listing of tag and index pricing. Note that the light-weight stocks have an upcharge. Also note the comparatively small difference in cost for comparable grades.

	1 carton 1 item	4 cartons assorted	16 cartons assorted	5M lb assorted
Tag Stock				
Manila sub 100	.4440	.3885	.3580	.2985
125 & up	.4265	.3735	.3440	.2835
White sub 100	.4485	.3925	.3615	.2985
125 & up	.4310	.3770	.3475	.2865
Ivory	.4575	.4000	.3685	.3045
Other Colors	.4750	.4155	.3825	.3165
Index Stock				
White sub 90	.4790	.4195	.3860	.3195
110 & up	.4615	.4040	.3720	.3075
Colors sub 90	.5065	.4430	.4080	.3375
110 & up	.4880	.4270	.3930	.3255

Vellum Bristol

The next category is bristol. It also has its confusing characteristics, we regret to say, but we have to discuss it realistically. There are several types of bristols.

First is the vellum bristol, a very bulky sheet, somewhat soft for a paper stock that is equivalent in bulk to a cover stock. The advantage is the high bulk for minimum weight. The disadvantage is the softness in a sheet that might be used as a cover stock. The basic size of this sheet is $22\frac{1}{2} \times 28\frac{1}{2}$. It can be bought in substance 67, 80, 100, and 120 lb basis.

In Table 5-10 we have listed the weights and carton packing. The blank spaces mean that certain basic weights are not available in every size. In colors, note the limitation of this mill making colors only in 67 lb basis, a situation that is not necessarily true of every mill.

Table 5-10. Vellum bristol sizes and weights available, with carton packing. Note the limitation of one weight only in colors. (This situation may vary with other mills.)

Substance →	WHITE VELLUM BRISTOL			
	67	80	100	120
22½ × 28½	134 (900)	160 (750)	200 (600)	240 (500)
23 × 35	168 (800)	201 (600)	252 (500)	302 (400)
26 × 40	216 (600)	260 (500)		
35 × 46	336 (500)			
Canary, Blue, Gold, Green, Ivory, Pink				
22½ × 28½	134 (900)			
23 × 35	168 (800)			
26 × 40	216 (600)			

The word "vellum" really denotes a rough finish as opposed to a smooth finish, for example. Yet there are other, higher-quality bristols that are more solid in manufacturing and less bulky, and have more strength characteristics, as well as whiteness. Besides vellum finish, they also come in smooth, satin finish, and felt finish, to name the most common. These high-quality bristols start with 100 lb basis in most cases.

Other bristols come pasted together, generally in double thickness. A few also come in rag content, to round out the picture.

Coated Bristol

Another important category of bristol is the coated type—coated one side and coated two sides. It is often referred to as coated cover bristol, since it is commonly used as an economical cover stock. The sheet is ideal for paperback books, the main purpose for which it was designed.

The coated bristols come in point thicknesses rather than the pound-per-ream basis weight. Nevertheless, the pricing structure calls for cost per pound. To help clarify this situation, please refer to the chart in Table 5-11. Notice the wide range of sizes available. This flexibility also allows for any grain direction and size. The same is true for the coated two sides (C2S) stock.

Table 5-11. Chart showing point thickness in thousandths of an inch (e.g., .008″) and the respective weights and carton packing for each.

| Substance → | COATED COVER BRISTOL C1S | | |
	8 Pt.	10 Pt.	12 Pt.
20 × 26	135 (1000)	163 (900)	195 (700)
23 × 29	173 (800)	208 (700)	251 (600)
23 × 35	209 (700)	252 (600)	302 (500)
26 × 40	270 (500)	326 (500)	390 (400)
35 × 46	418 (300)	504 (300)	604 (250)

In Table 5-12 we have shown the price structure. In this type of stock, 8 pt. is considered light-weight and therefore commands a higher price. The same situation holds true for C2S stock, with prices somewhat higher for the two-sided coating.

Table 5-12. Chart showing cost per pound of coated cover bristol C1S. Note that 8 pt. is considered light-weight in this instance. Also, these prices are *approximate*.

| | WHITE COATED COVER BRISTOL C1S per pound | | | |
	1 carton 1 item	4 cartons assorted	16 cartons assorted	5M lb 1 item
8 pt.	.5090	.4495	.4190	.3565
10 Pt. & up	.4575	.4040	.3765	.3200

Thus we conclude our discussion of how to purchase the major items of paper bought in *sheets*. There are many specialty papers and specialty covers that we have not discussed because of their less popular use.   Nevertheless we feel that sufficient background has been covered for the reader to continue to learn. Since paper merchants are the distribution source for many grades, the paper salesman's job is to assist a customer in making selections for a given purpose. On the other hand, the paper buyer should be familiar with the paper business as well, so that *the right questions can be asked. Learning is an endless process.*

Paper in Rolls

Paper is also purchased in rolls. There are small web presses that take narrow rolls, particularly the specialty webs. Larger presses that take wider webs are the most common types in the printing industry.

Newspapers are probably the largest users of roll paper. The nature of the printing operation demands it. Also, since web presses, which feed from rolls, print at high speeds, they consume large tonnage.

The next widely used roll paper is the machine coated type. This is the sort of paper used by the mass consumer publications, and many carloads are utilized in printing a single issue. On the other hand, with the improved technology in printing presses, many trade publications have switched from sheet-fed to web-fed printing despite their much shorter press requirements.

Purchasing paper in rolls is comparatively simple: the amount of paper in pounds, multiplied by the cost per pound, equals the paper bill. The next question is, how much paper must be bought for a specific job? Web printing plants have to know the answer to this question, for they live with it constantly. On the other hand, the purchasing agent had better be sure that the proper amount of paper is consumed because too often the paper is the most expensive single item that goes into a manufactured product. A monthly or weekly publication is an excellent example of such use.

Web Spoilage

One of the problems with web printing is to figure the correct amount of spoilage. Formulas sound fine, but the variables are many. Some of the factors affecting spoilage are:

1. *Cores and wrappers.* These are small items per roll, but they add up.
2. *Roll damage.* If the roll gets dropped for any reason, it may be dented. It is unwound until the layer is even again. Another factor is the possible biting of the roll-handling equipment into the roll itself. Once again the roll has to be unraveled until the paper is smooth once again.
3. *Makeready spoilage.* This is the largest single factor because register, ink color (even if only black), and proper folding are all part of the picture. This is where the greatest amount of paper is wasted.
4. *Web breaks.* When a web of paper breaks, the press is shut down immediately. All of the damaged paper has to be removed, and the web "rethreaded." This may upset some of the ink/water balance, in web offset, and more paper is wasted in getting back to par.
5. *Roll changes.* Many webs have to shut down, although briefly, for web changes. The flying paster, which is used to prevent press shutdown, is advantageous in this regard. The press may be slowed down momentarily while the new roll, which has been revolving at a rapid rate in preparation for joining, is placed in contact with the expended roll. This starts the new roll in the press run, while the old one is carefully removed. Approximately $\frac{1}{4}$ inch of paper is left on the old roll. This is additional spoilage.
6. *Color.* The more colors that are involved, the more items of registration there are that have to be checked before the actual run is started.

6
PAPER MATH

Although we have included a fair amount of math in discussing basis weights and weights for special sizes, there are many other items that are invaluable. They will be covered by tables, as well as actual examples.

After many years of teaching, and observing how quickly adults have forgotten basic arithmetic, I can only caution you that this book is not a novel—it should be read and reread where necessary. Make notes of special examples covered below—notes that will be meaningful to you when a similar situation arises. To do so will enhance the learning process, and give you maximum value from your reading.

Comparative Weights

The first table that you will find useful is the table of comparative weights, Table 6-1. Comparative weights can be important for many reasons, a few of which are shown below. Probably you will discover others.

Notice on the chart that 16 lb bond is equivalent to 40 lb offset, while 20 lb bond is equivalent to 50 lb offset, and 60 lb offset is equivalent to 24 lb bond. These simple examples can be important

Table 6-1. Comparative weight chart showing *approximately* the equivalent weights of the various papers.

Ledger Bond and 17 X 22	Book 25 X 38	Cover 20 X 26	Bristol 22½ X 28½	Index 20½ X 24¾	Index 25½ X 30½	Tag 24 X 36
12	30	—	—	—	—	—
13	33	—	—	—	—	—
16	40	—	—	—	—	—
20	50	—	—	—	—	—
24	60	—	—	—	—	—
28	70	—	—	—	—	—
32	80	—	—	—	—	—
36	90	50	—	—	—	—
40	100	—	67	—	—	—
—	110	60	—	59	90	100
—	120	65	80	—	—	—
—	—	—	—	72	110	125
—	—	80	100	—	—	—
—	—	90	—	—	—	150
—	—	—	—	91	140	—
—	—	100	120	—	—	—
—	—	—	130	—	—	175
—	—	120	150	—	—	200
—	—	130	160	—	—	—

if the paper you are looking for is not immediately available in the merchant's warehouse, and you don't have time to wait for an incoming shipment. Furthermore, you may need only a small quantity —perhaps less than a carton—which is another reason for substitution. Conversely, you may need a large quantity, and the merchant may have an inadequate supply on hand.

In bond papers, be careful if you are printing on both sides of the sheet. Be sure to check the opacity before making your decision. Colored papers generally have better opacity than their comparable grade in white. Obtaining samples before placing the order will help.

On the other hand, my experience tells me that the word "opacity" needs more than a passing explanation. Too often the novice will place a 50 lb sheet over some black, bold type and say there is too much show-through. Bear in mind that when type is printed on an ordinary offset paper, the backup of other type will offer an important opacity factor. To go to extremes by ordering special opaques, or heavier stock, or coated stock, may price the paper right out of the budget. Be realistic.

Referring again to Table 6-1, we have indicated the old and new index sizes. The index made is exactly the same as the chart indicates. Regarding cover stocks, there is some difference between coated and antique regarding bulk; basis weights are the same, by definition.

The comparative weight chart should be useful for purposes of identity, education, and paper substitution.

Bulk Chart

Bulk is an important factor in selecting paper. In Table 6-2 we have a chart showing bulk in thousandths of an inch, expressed to three or four decimal places. These figures are fairly accurate but *not exact*.

Now we shall take some paper problems and add a few variations. Once again, make notes in a way that will enable you to refer to this section when you encounter a similar situation. On the other hand, if you have sufficient paper-buying experience, and the examples given will be firmly implanted in your mind, so much the better.

Practical Problem

Job Problem: How much paper should be ordered for 10,000 catalogs, 160 pages and cover, $8\frac{1}{2} \times 11$, printed two colors inside, with a four-color front and back cover? Assume 70 lb coated inside, with an 80 lb coated cover. Also compute the paper cost.

Solution: Before the answer can be estimated, we must decide on press sizes. Then we have to take into account the proper amount of spoilage. Let us say we shall use a 35×45 sheet. This will give us 32 pages out of a sheet, a desired signature size. An alternative

Table 6-2. Chart showing bulk of various papers in thousandths of an inch. These figures will vary slightly with different mills.

BULKING CHART

	Basis	Caliper		Basis	Caliper
Bond			Tag		
17 × 22	13	.0025	24 × 36	100	.0075
	16	.003		125	.009
	20	.004		150	.011
	24	.0047		175	.0125
				200	.015
				250	.0175
Offset				300	.0225
25 × 38	40	.0032			
	50	.004	Uncoated Book,		
	60	.0045	Antique,		
	70	.005	25 × 38	50	.0045
	80	.006		60	.005
	100	.0075		70	.006
	120	.009		80	.0065
Coated Book			Bristol, Vellum		
25 × 38	60	.003	22½ × 28½	67	.0085
	70	.0035		80	.010
	80	.004		100	.011
	100	.0055		120	.0125
	120	.006			
			Cast Coated,		
Coated Cover			C2S Enamel		
20 × 26	50	.005	25 × 38	80	.004
	60	.006		100	.005
	65	.0065			
	80	.008	C1S Litho	60	.004
	100	.010		70	.0045
				80	.005
Cover, Antique			C2S Cover		
20 × 26	50	.007	20 × 26	65	.0066
	65	.009		80	.0083
	80	.0105		100	.0105
	100	.0135			
	130	.018	C1S Cover	50	.0048
				65	.0065
				80	.0085
Index					
25½ × 30½	90	.007			
	110	.008			
	140	.0105			

would be to use 23 X 35 paper, but this would double the number of signatures for binding, increasing the cost.

35 X 45 = 16 pages up, 32 pages per sheet

23 X 35 = 8 pages up, 16 pages per sheet

160 pages = 5 X 32, or 10 X 16

Since the inside is to be in two colors, we would allow 6% spoilage for printing and binding. Thus:

10,000 plus 6% =10,600 sheets per signature

Inasmuch as we have five signatures, the paper needed would be:

10,600 X 5 = 53,000 sheets of 35 X 45

35 X 45–232M

53,000 X 232M = 12,296 lb of inside stock

The next item is the cost. Refer to your merchant's catalog and you will find that the cost per pound in the 10,000 lb price bracket is $.3565 for a reasonably good grade. Using your handy calculator, you get:

12,296 X .3565 = $4,383.52

Referring to 80 lb cover stock, we find that the weight of 20 X 26 = 160M. Of course we will use 20 X 26, since the $8\frac{1}{2}$ X 11 cover has an open size of 11 X 17, plus trim and an allowance for the backbone, or spine. (We hope you already realize that a catalog of 160 pages would look better with a "square" back instead of a very difficult saddle stitch binding job.)

Since 20 X 26 will give us two covers out of a sheet, we need 5,000 sheets plus spoilage. With a four-color cover, 12% spoilage, or 600 sheets additional, is added to the basic requirement, totaling 5,600 sheets.

5,600 X 160M = 896 lb

Regarding the price structure, there may be two viewpoints. First, the quantity of cover stock falls into the four-carton, or 600 lb, bracket. On the other hand, since the cover and inside stock are being ordered at one time, making one shipment to one destination, let us assume the same price of $.3565 per lb.

$$896 \times .3565 = \$319.42$$

Adding $319.42 to $4,383.52, we have a total paper cost of $4,702.94.

Assuming that the cost of plates and press time for this requirement is equal to $6,000, the client is faced with an $11,000 expense, plus binding costs, and says it is out of his budget area. What can be done now? Let us consider some alternatives to lowering paper costs, a very sizable part of the manufacturing expenditure.

Alternate Solution

Since this is a catalog, it is possible that the pages can be made somewhat smaller without deleting any of the catalog items. Exploring this possibility, we refer to the chart of standard paper sizes and see that the next smaller paper size is 25 X 38. This would permit a trim page size of 6 X 9, with 16 pages on each side of the sheet, or 32-page signatures for binding.

Following the same procedure as we did for the $8\frac{1}{2}$ X 11 size, we will need 53,000 sheets of 25 X 38 paper.

$$25 \times 38 - 140M$$

$$53 \times 140 = 7,420 \text{ lb}$$

This time our paper bracket falls into the 5,000 lb category with a price of $.3885 per pound. Multiplying:

$$7,420 \times .3885 = \$2,882.67$$

This represents a sizable saving of approximately $1,500 in inside paper costs. Add to this an equal saving of at least $1,500 in press costs, and the saving is meaningful.

A Third Solution

Finally, there is a third approach to the problem. Assume that the

6 × 9 size is unsatisfactory and that $8\frac{1}{2}$ × 11, or possibly a fraction smaller, is the only acceptable format. Let us see what can be done about changing the paper.

Look at the "bulking chart" in Table 6-2 and observe that 70 lb coated bulks .0035 inch. In the offset category, 50 lb offset bulks .004″. This would be a regular or vellum finish. To substitute an offset stock, why not try a moderately priced 50 lb *opaque* offset, smooth finish if you prefer? The smooth sheet might bulk as low as .0035—the same as the coated—but use a lot less paper. The weight of the new stock now reads 35 × 45—166M. Therefore:

$$53 \times 166 = 8{,}798 \text{ lb}$$

Looking up the 5,000 lb bracket under a moderate opaque offset, we have a unit cost of $.3655 per lb.

$$8{,}798 \times .3655 = \$3{,}215.67$$

Already we have a saving approximating $1,100.00. A small additional saving can be obtained by substituting an 8 pt. coated bristol for the 8 pt. cover.

Using a little ingenuity and studying the situation thoroughly might even bring other cost-saving ideas into the picture.

Postage Factors

Let us now approach another phase of paper math by considering a large item of related costs—postage. Somehow, we can use all of our ingenuity to save money, but when it comes to mailing, there is no room for bargaining.

Problem: A 48-page catalog, $8\frac{1}{2}$ × 11, printed in two colors on 70 lb coated stock, self cover, is to be mailed individually at third class postage rates; total quantity: 8,000 copies. Determine cost of paper plus postage.

Solution: A logical solution is to use a 23 × 35 sheet, which yields 16 pages when printed on both sides. The catalog will use three sheets of paper, or three signatures for binding. The decision for self cover means that there will not be a separate cover, usually of heavier stock. The cover, if used, would add press, cover stock, and binding charges to the job, besides some added weight.

Here is the arithmetic:

$$23 \times 35-119M \text{ for } 16 \text{ pages}$$

Allowing a spoilage factor of 500 sheets per form:

$$8,500 \times 3 \text{ forms} = 25,500 \text{ sheets}$$

$$25.5 \times 119M = 3,035 \text{ lb of paper to be bought}$$

The ton price of the paper is \$.4690 per pound.

$$3,035 \times .4690 = \$1,423.42 \text{ total cost of paper}$$

Now we introduce another factor to our paper math: what is the cost of postage per catalog? Before we can answer that question we must know the weight of each catalog.

One easy answer is to call the paper merchant and have him make up a dummy of 48 pages of your stock and weigh it. Nice work if you can get it done as quickly as you want it. Perhaps you are miles away from the merchant, and he has to make up the book and mail it. That introduces other time problems. Even if you live in a large metropolis, you can't expect someone to drop everything to take care of your request. Then, when the dummy is made up, it takes time to have a messenger make the delivery. Time is not in your favor in any case.

A more painful, but surer, way is to resort to your calculator and figure it out. Here is some more mind-boggling arithmetic. One solution is given below, following the logic of our earlier descriptions.

$$
\begin{array}{ll}
8\frac{1}{2} \times 11 & \\
\underline{4 \ \times \ 2} & \text{(8 pages up)} \\
34 \ \times 22 & \text{(trim size of 16 pages)}
\end{array}
$$

For those not acquainted with book work, we suggest that you take a piece of paper and fold it in half, again in half, then finally in half again. Make each fold at right angles to the previous one, for a total of three folds. If you have followed these simple directions correctly, open up the sheet and you will notice that you have eight panels--four across and two deep, for a total of eight. Eight pages on each side means sixteen printed pages out of the sheet. If you were con used before this, the situation should be clear to you now. (See Figure 6-1.)

Please do not read on till you have mastered this simple step. Keep going over it until you have digested it, then study its relationship to Figure 6-1.

16-Page Signature

Fold the paper back again on the creases and hold the last folded edge in your left hand. You are now holding what is known as a 16-page signature. Also note that you have closed edges on the top and right-hand side. These are opened up by trimming the top, bottom, and outside edges. In our example, the objective would be to obtain a finished trim size of $8\frac{1}{2} \times 11$. To complete the picture technically, three signatures would be collated and stitched (wire stapled) before the final trims were made. The purpose of stapling before trimming is to ensure that you have a complete catalog which will not fall apart. You can simulate this binding operation by taking a scissors and trimming the three sides as discussed.

Now that you have done that, refer once again to the arithmetic above, and all of the elements should fall logically into place.

The next question is, what is the weight of the 22 X 34 trim size? Using the same type of arithmetic as in the previous chapter, we have the following equation:

$$\frac{23 \times 35}{22 \times 34} = \frac{119}{x}$$

The letter x is the M weight we are trying to obtain.

$$x = \frac{119 \times (22 \times 34)}{23 \times 35}$$

$$x = 111 \text{ lb per M sheets}$$

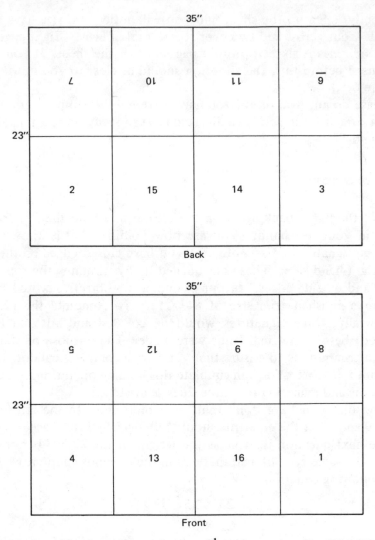

Figure 6-1. Imposition for a 16-page signature, $8\frac{1}{2} \times 11$ page size. The 23" × 35" sheet, when printed on both sides and folded as suggested in the text, will be numbered consecutively from 1 to 16. (Note: if the numbers do not fall into place, refold the sheet in the opposite direction.)

This is logical. If 23 × 35 weighs 119M, 22 × 34, which is slightly smaller in size, should weigh less. It does. In other words, we have now printed the paper and trimmed it to final size, and are trying to calculate the *exact* weight. Since there are 16 ounces to a pound, and since postage costs are determined in ounces, we have to convert our figures correspondingly.

Three sheets per catalog are equal to 333 lb per thousand catalogs, or .333 lb per single catalog. Multiplying by 16, we get 5.328 ounces, rounded to 5.3 ounces.

Postage Costs

Postage costs, at this writing, are $.34 each, since the weight falls into the "4 to 6 ounce" category. Multiplying by 8,000 catalogs, the mailing totals $2,720.00.

In summary:

$$
\begin{aligned}
\text{Paper cost} &= \$1,423.42 \\
\text{Postage} &= \underline{2,720.00} \\
\text{Paper \& postage} &\quad \$4,143.42
\end{aligned}
$$

The postage costs are overwhelming. The only way to reduce them is to try to get a lighter paper and hope we can reach the next lower bracket—$.24 in the "2 to 4 ounce" category. If that is possible, 8,000 catalogs would incur a postage bill of $1,920.00.

Trying Lighter-Weight Paper

Let us try a 50 lb opaque sheet. The lighter weight with a bright white paper is closest to the coated stock we have put aside. The advantage of the opaque paper is that it gives better reflectivity and ink holdout, the next best alternative.

As in the previous problem, we are now trying to find both paper costs and trimmed book weight for postage purposes.

23 × 35—85M

Following the preceding discussion, we shall again use 8,500 sheets per form, which, multiplied by 3 forms, again gives us a total of 25,500 sheets. Continuing from this point:

$$25.5 \times 85M = 2,168 \text{ lb}$$

There are many grades of opaque just as there are many grades of coated stock. For our purposes we shall assume a per-pound cost of $.4560 as being reasonable.

$$2,168 \times .4560 = \$988.61$$

Now we must find the weight of the new catalog using 50 lb stock. We shall use the same mathematical approach with a different twist. If you find it difficult to understand, please reread! We shall now find the weight of a single sheet of $8\frac{1}{2} \times 11$, called x in the following equation:

$$\frac{23 \times 35}{8\frac{1}{2} \times 11} = \frac{85}{x}$$

$$x = \frac{85(8\frac{1}{2} \times 11)}{25 \times 35}$$

$$x = 9.1 \text{ lb per M sheets}$$

One $8\frac{1}{2} \times 11 = .0091$ lb per sheet

$$.0091 \text{ lb} \times 16 \text{ ounces} = .15 \text{ ounces per sheet}$$

Our catalog contains 48 pages, or 48 printed sides, which constitutes 24 pieces of $8\frac{1}{2} \times 11$. To avoid confusion, we might call them 24 leaves. Therefore:

$$24 \times .15 = 3.6 \text{ ounces per catalog}$$

Summarizing the new costs using 50 lb stock, we have:

$$
\begin{aligned}
\text{Paper cost} &= \$ \ \ \ 988.61 \\
\text{Postage} &= \underline{\ 1,920.00} \\
\text{Total} &= \$2,906.61
\end{aligned}
$$

We have succeeded in reducing the postage weight to just under 4 ounces. To play it safe, I would shave the catalog $\frac{1}{16}$ inch at least to be sure there is no slip or unforeseen element. After all, if you are wrong, 8,000 X .10 = $800 lost!

Knowledge is the greatest aid to ingenuity. Let us look into some of the problems that occur with cover stock.

Greeting Cards

Many greetings cards or business announcements require a deckle edge. In cover stock you can safely assume that if a certain grade comes with a deckle edge, the paper size will be 26 X 40 and the deckle will be in the 40 inch dimension.

Problem: A printer stocks greeting announcements, size $9\frac{1}{4}$ X 12, and his stock is low and needs to be replaced. The card must have a deckle edge on the 12″ dimension. Although the requirement is small, an even carton, containing 500 sheets of cover stock, will be purchased. How many cards can be cut out of the carton?

Solution: Because of the deckle edge, it is safest to make a diagram and not rely on simple arithmetic (see Figure 6-2).

Note that in Figure 6-2A we have six units out, but in Figure 6-2B we can cut eight units out with much less waste. The paper waste is unfortunate but has to be taken into consideration in the cost. In Figure 6-2A, note that we have shown the waste in the middle of the sheet rather than at the bottom. We must have a 12″ deckle edge; therefore the paper must be cut as illustrated.

To complete the problem, 500 multiplied by 6 will yield 3,000 pieces. This figure will be reduced slightly by a spoilage factor in printing and folding.

$8\frac{1}{2}$ X 11 Units of Cover Stock

While we are talking about cover stock, another problem, quite common, is to cut $8\frac{1}{2}$ X 11 units out of a sheet. Often a specification requiring a special color and texture will mean that the cover paper will only be available in 80 lb cover weight and a size of

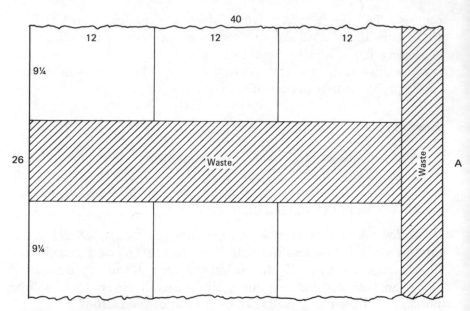

Figure 6-2. (A) Diagram showing six units out, with considerable waste because of the deckle-edge requirements. (B) Diagram showing eight units out with much less waste, but unsuitable because of the deckle-edge requirements.

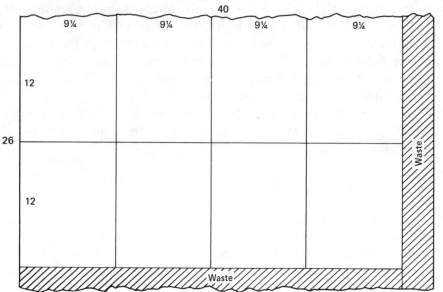

26 X 40. How many units can be cut out of a sheet? (There are no deckle-edge requirements.)

Arithmetically:

$$26 \times 40$$
$$8\tfrac{1}{2} \times 11$$

Answer A:

$$4 \times \ 8\tfrac{1}{2} = 34$$
$$2 \times 11 \ \ = 22$$

or 8 units out of a sheet

Answer B:

$$3 \times \ 8\tfrac{1}{2} = 25\tfrac{1}{2}$$
$$3 \times 11 \ \ = 33$$

or 9 units out of a sheet

In answer A we get eight units out of a sheet with the grain direction in the $8\tfrac{1}{2}''$ dimension. The waste is considerable, as shown in Figure 6-3A. This may be unavoidable if the grain direction is mandatory. On the other hand, if it is only a matter of folding, a good solid score might do just as well.

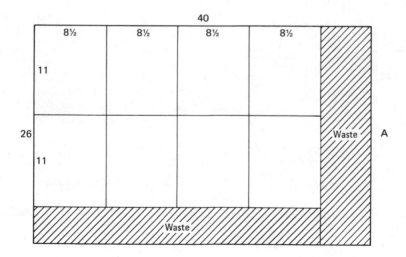

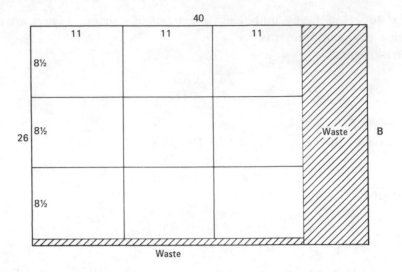

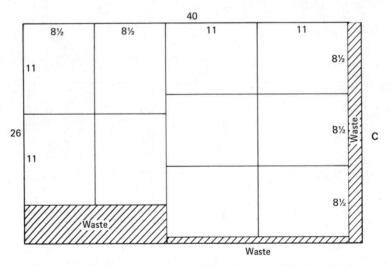

Figure 6-3. (A) Eight units out of a sheet. (B) Nine units out of a sheet. (C) Ten units out of a sheet.

In answer B we have changed the grain direction to the 11″ dimension and gotten nine units out of the sheet, with less waste. Regardless of grain, if the paper has to be folded, it will require scoring as a preliminary operation because the stock is too heavy.

If you are content to settle for answer B because you can get an additional $12\frac{1}{2}\%$, then you are still not quite right. The arithmetic was a tool for a quick answer. Sometimes a diagram such as the one shown in Figure 6-3C will reveal a more ingenious solution—ten units out. Of course the grain is crossed, meaning that you have two different grain directions. For economy, you just can't beat it. With expensive stock like 80 lb cover, no solution should be left untried.

Paper Multiples

At this point we would like to offer a suggestion regarding how to find the proper size of paper that might be used. Note the following listings:

$$2 \times 2 = 4 \qquad 2 \times 8 = 16$$
$$2 \times 4 = 8 \qquad 4 \times 8 = 32$$
$$4 \times 4 = 16 \qquad 8 \times 8 = 64$$

Also:

$$3 \times 8 = 24 \qquad 4 \times 6 = 24 \qquad 8 \times 6 = 48$$

If you are not familiar with impositions, the figures shown probably mean nothing. We'll try to shed light on the matter with some illustrations. However, if you are interested in delving more deeply into the subject, my book entitled *Production Planning and Impositions Simplified* (North American Publishing Co.) will help greatly.

Let us start off with the common size, $8\frac{1}{2} \times 11$, and see how the multiples help arrive at a paper size.

$8\frac{1}{2} \times 11$	$8\frac{1}{2} \times 11$	$8\frac{1}{2} \times 11$
2×2	2×4	4×4
17×22	34×22	34×44
A.	B.	C.

In item A we have an easy answer, multiplying each dimension by two, printing four pages up. When we back up the form with an additional four pages, we have an eight-page signature for folding and binding. Since we have to trim off at least $\frac{1}{8}$ inch from the top, bottom, and side, think of an *untrimmed* size of $8\frac{5}{8} \times 11\frac{1}{4}$ ($8\frac{1}{2} + \frac{1}{8} = 8\frac{5}{8}$; $11 + \frac{1}{8} + \frac{1}{8} = 11\frac{1}{4}$).

In item B we must establish a simple rule: always multiply the smaller dimension by the larger number, the larger dimension by the smaller number. To convince yourself, try it the other way and see what a ridiculous-size sheet you will come up with.

In item C, the multiples are even.

Referring to standard size paper, we have $17\frac{1}{2} \times 22\frac{1}{2}$, 23×35, 35×45. These sizes work out very well in our multiples, since we must add our trim area in any case. This should prove helpful to those who are not at all familiar with how to arrive at a quick answer in finding the right-size paper for a given job.

$8\frac{1}{2} \times 11$	$8\frac{1}{2} \times 11$	$8\frac{1}{2} \times 11$
2×8	4×8	8×8
22×68	44×68	68×88
D.	E.	F.

Multiple Trial and Error

Items in the next set of multiples do not work as well as the first set. In item D, the proportion does not fit, and so D must be discarded as unusable.

Item E is usable for the right press. Adding the necessary trims, a 45×70 sheet is realistic. There are presses of a 52×76 or slightly larger size that make this paper practical. To go a bit further, the 45×70 sheet, printing 32 pages up and 32 pages on the backup, delivers 64 pages. This signature is too big and more often than not, it would be slit *on the press* to deliver two separate 32's for folding.

Item F is out of the question. There are no sheet sizes as such and no presses large enough to handle them.

$8\frac{1}{2} \times 11$	$8\frac{1}{2} \times 11$	$8\frac{1}{2} \times 11$
$\underline{3 \quad \times \; 8}$	$\underline{4 \quad \times \; 6}$	$\underline{6 \quad \times \; 8}$
33 X 68	44 X 51	66 X 68
G.	H.	I.

In our last series of multiples, item G, while not standard, is possible if sheeted, let us say, to 35 X 70. This can be shaved to 35 X 69 if there are no bleed pages and there is a 69″ press that can handle this size easily. If that were the case, after printing front and back we would have a 48-page signature for binding. This is also too large and would have to be cut in half and folded as two 24's.

Item H is also feasible on a large enough press. The comments on the preceding item also hold for this one.

Item I is totally unusable for the same reasons discussed in item F.

Size $5\frac{1}{2} \times 8\frac{1}{2}$ Multiples

The trial-and-error method is interesting and sound in its approach. Let us try the same situation with other sizes.

$5\frac{1}{2} \times 8\frac{1}{2}$	$5\frac{1}{2} \times 8\frac{1}{2}$	$5\frac{1}{2} \times 8\frac{1}{2}$
$\underline{2 \quad \times \; 2}$	$\underline{2 \quad \times \; 4}$	$\underline{4 \quad \times \; 4}$
11 X 17	17 X 22	22 X 34
J.	K.	L.

Work and Turn Forms

Now that we have halved the $8\frac{1}{2} \times 11$, item J would have to be run on a small press. Or, if the run were large enough, it could be run work and turn, or two up work and turn. Those who are puzzled by this terminology should please refer to Figure 6-4. Here you will see a form that is printed, then turned like the leaves of a book, and printed by the same plate. In this manner, page 3 will be backed up by page 4, page 6 by page 5, and so on. It not only works—it is a common method of printing. However, the printed sheet must be

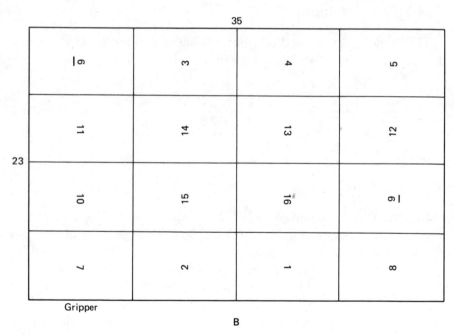

Figure 6-4. (A) Eight-page work-and-turn form for $5\frac{1}{2} \times 8\frac{1}{2}$ page size. (B) Sixteen-page work-and-turn form for $5\frac{1}{2} \times 8\frac{1}{2}$ page size.

cut in half before folding, and both parts will be exactly alike. This effects a saving in both platemaking and presswork.

One of the common problems in work-and-turn printing, or even two up work and turn, is miscalculation of the amount of paper needed. The common error in estimating paper requirements is to double the amount actually needed, or perhaps to halve it. In other words, if the printing requirement calls for 10,000 copies, and the paper is being printed work and turn, 5,000 sheets plus spoilage is the proper amount to order.

The diagram in Figure 6-4A would pertain to item J. Do not forget that four up in printing means eight pages for binding. There are two sides to every sheet of paper.

Likewise item K is portrayed as a work-and-turn form by printing eight pages up for each side, for a total of sixteen pages. After printing, this sheet would also be cut in half before folding.

Sheetwise Form

Item L is a logical candidate for a 23 × 35 sheet. This would yield two 16-page forms for printing and one 32-page form for binding. To distinguish between items K and L, we might refer to L as a "sheetwise" form. (See Figure 6-5.)

$$
\begin{array}{ccc}
5\frac{1}{2} \times 8\frac{1}{2} & 5\frac{1}{2} \times 8\frac{1}{2} & 5\frac{1}{2} \times 8\frac{1}{2} \\
\underline{2 \times 8} & \underline{4 \times 8} & \underline{8 \times 8} \\
17 \times 44 & 34 \times 44 & 44 \times 68 \\
\\
\text{M.} & \text{N.} & \text{P.}
\end{array}
$$

Item M is impractical because of the wide variation in sizes. To double the 17″ dimension, printing two up, gives us the same effect as N.

Item N is interesting because a 35 × 45 sheet, adding the necessary trims, is very much standard. This produces a 64-page form for binding, it seems. This is too thick a form, but there are two solutions. One is to cut the sheet in half and fold it as two 32's. A better way is to fold it as a *double 32*. This means that the sheet would enter the folding machine without precutting and get slit on the folder,

35

14	3	2	15
19	30	31	18
22	27	26	23
11	9	7	10

23 (left side)

Gripper

Back

while also being folded as two 32's. This is more sensible, and more economical.

Item P is logical only for a very large press. It could be slit on the press, if possible, during printing.

$$5\tfrac{1}{2} \times 8\tfrac{1}{2}$$
$$\underline{3 \quad \times \quad 8}$$
$$44 \quad \times 25\tfrac{1}{2}$$

Q.

$$5\tfrac{1}{2} \times 8\tfrac{1}{2}$$
$$\underline{4 \quad \times \quad 6}$$
$$33 \quad \times 34$$

R.

$$5\tfrac{1}{2} \times 8\tfrac{1}{2}$$
$$\underline{6 \quad \times \quad 8}$$
$$44 \quad \times 51$$

S.

Items Q, R, and S are rather poor candidates but not impossible. They can be sheeted specially, but none of the sizes are near standard.

To avoid monotony, we will end this type of arithmetic. If we were to continue, 6 X 9 and 7 X 10 sizes would be the next logical candidates. Other special sizes can also be used. The important thing to remember is how to use the multiple formulas and see how they fit. When you do, don't forget to *add* the $\tfrac{1}{8}$ inch trims on top, bottom, and side. In our illustrations we only used the trim sizes.

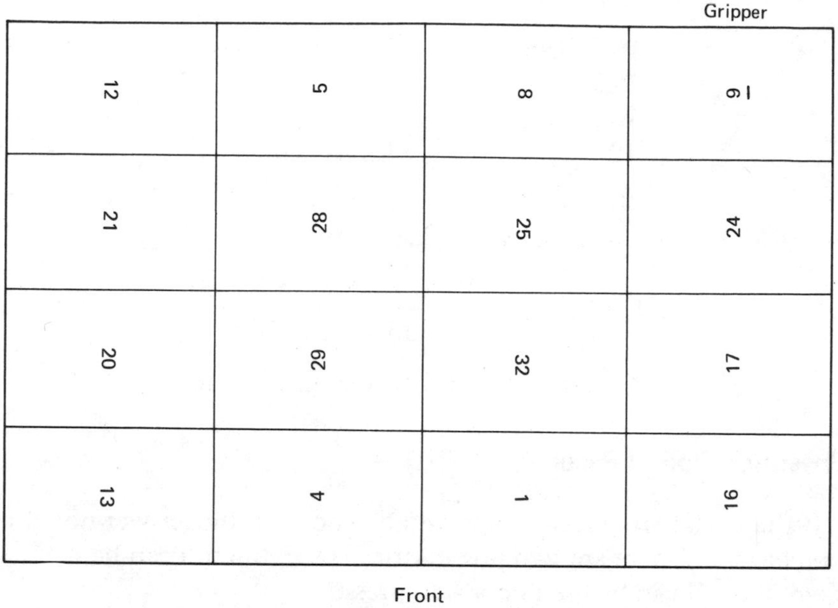

Gripper

12	5	8	9 I
21	28	25	24
20	29	32	17
13	4	1	16

Front

Figure 6-5. A 32-page sheetwise form showing front and back imposition. Note the gripper positions. If you can visualize both gripper sides being pushed together, with a hinge to join them, swing the back form on the hinge, and notice how the pages back up each other.

Linear Feet in a Roll of Paper

Now it is time to say a brief word about paper in rolls. To find the amount of linear feet in a roll, we have the following formula:

$$\text{Linear feet} = \frac{\text{Weight of roll} \times \text{Basis size} \times \text{Ream}}{\text{Width of roll} \times 12'' \times \text{Basis weight}}$$

A practical example would be to find how many feet (how much yardage, if you prefer) are contained in a roll of paper, 70 lb coated weighing 1,000 lb. The width of the roll is 35 inches.

We have the following known items:

Weight of roll	1,000 lb
Basis size	25 X 38 inches
Ream	500 sheets
Width of roll	35 inches
12"	Equals one foot
Basis weight	70 lb

Substituting, the equation would read:

$$\text{Linear feet} = \frac{1000 \times 25 \times 38 \times 500}{35 \times 12 \times 70}$$

Linear feet = 16,156 feet in the roll

Sheeting a Roll of Paper

Perhaps you are puzzled as to what to do with the answer now that you have it. There are two possibilities. One, the roll can be sheeted. Two, the roll can be used on a web press.

If the roll is to be sheeted, let us assume that it will be converted to 35 X 45. This procedure is simple: convert the feet to inches and divide by 45 to determine the number of sheets.

16,156 feet = 193,872 inches

$$\frac{193,872}{45} = 4,308 \text{ sheets}$$

Since there is bound to be some waste, we could optimistically expect approximately 4,000 sheets.

Calculating Signatures

Regarding the second question, what would be the yield of the 35 inch web of paper used on a press with a $22\frac{3}{4}$ " cutoff? Assuming that we are referring to folded signatures from the web, with a page size of $8\frac{3}{8} \times 10\frac{7}{8}$, we would get eight pages on each side to yield a sixteen-page folded signature.

The arithmetic:

$$\frac{193,872}{22.75} = 8,522 \text{ signatures (gross)}$$

From this we must deduct web press spoilage, which consists of the core, the paper left on the roll, makeready waste—all totaling perhaps 18%. This would leave an approximate net of 6,988. Rounding, we might approximate 7,000 sixteen-page folded signatures.

In conclusion, we have given considerable arithmetic in this chapter. We hope you have used a pocket or other calculator extensively to verify the answers. Once you have mastered the principles, by all means look for short-cut factors to speed up some of the solutions. It is to be hoped that in the decade of the 1980s our small-computer technology will enable us to have desk-top computers so designed as to permit feeding in some of the data for instant answers on a video display terminal. This is a logical possibility in graphic arts estimating.

7
PAPER METRICS

Despite the fact that the United States is the most industrialized nation with the world's highest living standards, it is the only major country in the world that still uses an antiquated system of weights and measures.

Centuries ago, when man found the need for a system of measurement, he resorted to parts of the body. A foot was the length of the king's foot. A yard was the distance from the tip of his nose to the end of his outstretched arm. Time was measured from the moon, sun, and stars.

SI

Now we are about to join the rest of the world in conforming to the International System of Units by using the metric system. This standard is known by the abbreviation SI.

In the graphic arts industry we are primarily concerned with grams and meters as measurements of weight and size. Our paper basis will be greatly simplified and expressed as a *simple unit of measurement* — the weight (grams) of a single sheet of paper that measures one meter square.

No longer will we be plagued with using a ream as the unit of quantity when we find it easier to order, and bill, on the basis of thousands of sheets. The basic sizes of 17 × 22, 25 × 38, 24 × 36, 22½ × 28½, 20 × 26, and others will eventually fade into oblivion as we accept a single uniform standard—the weight of a single sheet of paper, one meter square, expressed as grams per square meter. The symbol is g/m^2.

Grams per Square Meter

For example, 16 lb bond will now have a grammage (basis weight) of 60 g/m^2, and 50 lb offset will be expressed as 74 g/m^2. Newsprint, which is now expressed as 30 lb on a basis of 24 × 36 inches in size and a ream in quantity, will now be equated with 49 g/m^2.

To many of our readers, this may be a sudden plunge into cold water, unexpectedly and with the same degree of enthusiasm. The introduction of a whole new system may seem frightening at first, but this uneasiness will change very rapidly and much more quickly than you think. Furthermore, a dual system of present and future usage will be utilized to enhance the learning process.

Metric Decimals

The metric system has the advantage of being a decimal system. Using the *meter* as a basis of length, prefixes in multiples of 10 will be used. Using the gram as a measure of weight, the same standards will be used. Note the use of prefixes in the table below:

1 kilo = 1000	1 kilometer = 1000 meters
*1 hecto = 100	*1 hectometer = 100 meters
*1 deka = 10	*1 dekameter = 10 meters
1 = 1	1 meter = 1 meter
*1 deci = 0.1	*1 decimeter = 0.1 meter
1 centi = 0.01	1 centimeter = 0.01 meter
1 milli = 0.001	1 millimeter = 0.001 meter

We have added asterisks (*) to three items above to indicate that these terms are rarely used. Also, if we were to substitute "grams" for "meters," the same prefixes would apply. Read these prefixes just once more, and you will have mastered them.

Note the method of writing units, or decimals less than 1. A *0* is placed to the left of the decimal point, followed by the number in question. Another simple rule is the elimination of the comma to separate figures with more than three digits. For example:

$$1\ 000\ \text{km} \quad \text{or} \quad 10\ 000\ \text{kg}$$

Punctuation Eliminated

We have properly shown how to write an abbreviation for one thousand kilometers and ten thousand kilograms. All punctuation has been eliminated: no comma to separate the digits in units of three, and no period after the standard abbreviations. Also note that the same abbreviation pertains to both singular and plural.

The next thing to know is, how heavy is a gram and how long is a meter? The gram is very light—0.0353 ounce. Or, if you wish, there are 28 grams in one ounce. The meter is equal to 39.37 inches—slightly more than a yard.

A good way to think of these new terms is to refer to an ordinary paper clip. A paper clip weighs about 1 gram, while the thickness of the same clip is about 1 mm (one millimeter) or $\frac{1}{1000}$ meters.

Since the gram is so light, we often refer to kilograms as a unit of weight, with 1 kg equal to approximately 2.2 lb. Incidentally, talking about kilograms, there are 1 000 kg in a metric ton. The metric ton in turn is equal to 1.1 (short) tons—the ton that we now refer to as 2,000 lb.

Although not referring directly to paper, the unit of liquid volume will be the liter (abbreviated *l*). One liter is equal to 1.06 quarts.

Easy Metric Comparisons

We'll get into the exact figures later in our metrics. In the meantime, here are some rules of thumb to help you remember, or understand, the new terminology.

Table 7-1. Common conversions using exact multiples.

Symbol	When You Know	Multiply by	To Find	Symbol
in	inches	25.4	millimeters	mm
ft	feet	0.304 8	meters	m
yd	yards	0.914 4	meters	m
mi	miles	1.609 34	kilometers	km
yd^2	square yards	0.836 127	square meters	m^2
oz	ounces	28.349 5	grams	g
lb	pounds	0.453 592	kilograms	kg
mm	millimeters	0.039 370 1	inches	in
m	meters	3.280 84	feet	ft
m	meters	1.093 61	yards	yd
km	kilometers	0.621 371	miles	mi
m^2	square meters	1.195 99	square yards	yd^2
g	grams	0.035 274	ounces	oz
kg	kilograms	2.204 62	pounds	lb

A *meter* is a bit *more* than a yard.

A *kilogram* is a bit *more* than two pounds.

A *metric ton* is a bit *more* than a (short) ton.

A *liter* is a bit *more* than a quart.

A paper clip weighs *1 gram* ($\frac{1}{28}$ of an ounce).

A paper clip is *1 mm* thick ($\frac{1}{25}$ of an inch).

Obviously 1 gram and 1 millimeter are very small units. For this reason we round out the figures to the nearest whole number for purposes of discussion. When *exact* calculations are important, by all means use the fractions—and your calculator.

For example, when you want to convert inches to millimeters, multiply by 25.4. When you need to convert ounces to grams, you multiply by 28.349 5.

$$8\tfrac{1}{2} \text{ inches} \times 25.4 = 215.9 \text{ mm} \quad (216 \text{ mm rounded})$$

$$16 \text{ ounces} \times 28.349\ 5 = 453.592 \text{ g} \quad (454 \text{ g rounded})$$

See Table 7-1 for some common conversions.

Basis Weights And Grams Per Square Meter

17"x22"	20"x26"	22½"x28½"	25½"x30½"	23"x35"	24"x36"	25"x·38"	grams per square meter g/m²
x					x	20	30
9					x	x	34
x					x	24	36
11					x	x	41
x					x	30	44
13					30	33	49
x					x	35	52
15					x	x	56
x					x	40	59
16					x	x	60
x					40	x	65
x					x	45	67
x					x	50	74
20					x	x	75
x					50	x	81
x					x	60	89
24					x	x	90
x					60	x	98
x					x	70	104
28					x	x	105
x	40				x	x	108
x	x				70	x	114
x	x				x	80	118
32	x				x	x	120
x	x				80	x	130
x	x	x			x	90	133
36	50	x			x	x	135
x	x	67			90	x	146
x	x	x			x	x	147
x	x	x			x	100	148
40	x	x	x	x	x	x	150
x	60	x	x	x	x	x	162
x	x	x	90	x	100	x	163
x	x	80	x	100	x	x	175
x	65	x	x	x	x	x	176
	70	x	x	x	x	120	178
	x	90	x	x	x	x	189
	x	x	x	x	x	x	197
	x	x	110	x	x	x	199
	x	x	x	x	125	x	203
	80	x	x	x	x		216
	x	x	x	125	x		218
	x	100	x	x	x		219
	x	x	x	x	150		244
	x	x	140	x	x		253
	x	x	x	150	x		262
	x	120	x	x	x		263
	100	x	x	x	x		270
	x	x	x	x	175		285
	x	x	x	175	x		306
	x	140	170	x	x		307
	x	x	x	x	200		325
	x	x	x	200	x		349
	x	160	x	x	x		351
	130	x	x	x	x		352
		180	x		x		395
		x	220		x		398
		x	x		250		407
		200	x		x		438

Conversion Factors

In the future, our computation of the number of pounds of paper in a given lot or order will be expressed in kilograms. In the case of large quantities of paper, the terminology will be in metric tons. Here are some conversion factors that will be helpful:

To Convert:

Symbol	From	To	Symbol	Multiply by
lb	pounds	kilograms	kg	0.453 6
lb	pounds	metric tons	t	0.000 453 6
	short tons	metric tons	t	0.907 2

In Figure 7-1 you will find a chart that you will refer to quite often. This chart shows the most common basis weight sizes, and under each appropriate column will be basis weight numbers. The number in the right-hand column, moving horizontally across the page, will be the new weight basis expressed in grams per square meter (g/m^2).

Equivalents

This should be referred to as more than just a conversion chart—it should be a tool for possible paper substitution and understanding. Some examples are as follows:

1. 16 lb bond (17 × 22 bs) is just one gram heavier than 40 lb book paper. Since a gram is only $\frac{1}{28}$ of an ounce in weight, it would be correct to assume that the weights are equal.
2. 65 lb cover (basis 20 × 26) is just 1 gram heavier than 80 lb bristol. The "grammage" is about equal.
3. By interpolation, 110 lb coated paper is about equal to 60 lb coated cover.
4. 110 lb index (bs $25\frac{1}{2}$ × $30\frac{1}{2}$) is just a bit lighter than 125 lb tag (4 grams lighter, to be exact, or $\frac{1}{7}$ of an ounce).

Figure 7-1. Chart showing basis weights and grams per square meter. (*Courtesy American Paper Institute*)

Metric Labels

During this transition period, the paper companies will use labels showing metric and nonmetric identification. A typical example is shown in Figure 7-2.

The figures 23 × 35 are about three times the size of the metric description. Paper sizes will be shown metrically in millimeters, while the "grammage" or basis weight will be shown as grams per square meter. Other paper descriptions will be at the option of the paper manufacturers.

One question often asked is: "What will be the effect of our paper sizes when we go metric?" The answer is, "None." We shall continue to use our standard paper sizes as we use them today. As we have pointed out, our sizes, presently quoted only in inches, will eventually be designated in millimeters. Our basis weights, with many size standards and identified as the weight in pounds per 500 sheets, will disappear. In its place will be "grammage" as shown in Figure 7-1.

Of course we shall still refer to paper as cover, offset, coated book, tag, index, and the like. Our grammage will have a uniform basis: the weight of one sheet, one meter square.

BRIGHT WHITE OFFSET

23 × 35 – 102M · $^{S}_{U}_{B}$**60** REGULAR FINISH

584 × 889 mm   89 g/m^2

BRIGHT PAPER COMPANY • Big Creek, WA

Figure 7-2. Typical label on a carton of paper showing both metric and non-metric sizes. Note the substance expressed in terms of grams per square meter (g/m^2).

What else can we say about metrication? The paper industry has decided that it is not feasible to change basic paper sizes as we know them—but only to designate them metrically. However, we think it might be interesting to know what the British have decided. Since the United States is about to join the rest of the world in using the SI system, perhaps there will be an occasion to know what our neighbors across the ocean are using.

A0 System

Great Britain uses a size system known as A0. So do other countries. The system has some merit, as you will see from the following description.

By definition, an A0 sheet of paper is a rectangle that is 1 square meter in size. Half of A0 is A1, with an area of $\frac{1}{2}$ of a square meter. Half of A1 is A2, or $\frac{1}{4}$ of a square meter. This equal division continues to A10. An example of this is shown in Figure 7-3.

Using this standardization, one basic size, A0, can be cut into many smaller sizes. On the other hand, if a larger size is to be used, there is 2 A0. This size is, as you can readily guess, 2 meters square.

Measured in millimeters, the A0 size is 841 × 1189 mm. A1 measures 594 × 841 mm. Of course you realize we are rounding out fractions of a millimeter. In inches, A1 is equal to 23.39 × 33.11 inches.

As we said above, the United States will not follow the A0 system. An interesting question might be, "What is the nearest size to $8\frac{1}{2}$ × 11?" It would be A4, measuring 210 × 297 millimeters. Converted to inches, the size would be approximately $8\frac{1}{4}$ × $11\frac{3}{4}$.

Still another question comes to mind. The thickness of paper is often expressed in "points." By this we mean that 4-pt. thickness is equal to .004 inch. How shall we replace this measurement metrically? This problem is not difficult, since the metric system is a decimal system. For example:

$$1 \text{ inch} = 25.4 \text{ mm}$$

$$.001 \text{ inch} = 0.025 \text{ 4 mm}$$

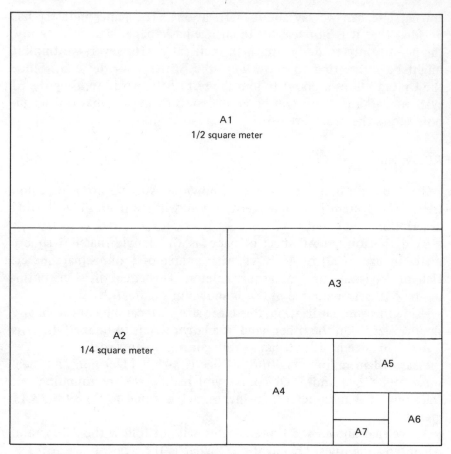

Figure 7-3. The A0 system is based on the fact that A0 equals 1 square meter. Half of A0, called A1, is $\frac{1}{2}$ of a square meter. A2 is half of A1, and so on.

Micro Prefix

For the purpose of simplifying fractions we now have to resort to a new definition. The prefix "milli" means one thousandth; one millimeter represents one thousandth of a meter. Since the millimeter is too large a unit to indicate paper thickness, we can readily see that we need an equivalent for thousandths of an inch. The prefix we shall refer to is "micro," which means one millionth. This fits the pattern well by using the word "micrometer." A micrometer represents one millionth of a meter, or one thousandth of a millimeter.

In the above equation, we might, for example, say that one point of thickness is equal to 25.4 micrometers. Once again, since the unit is small, we shall round out the fraction and say that 1 pt. equals 25 micrometers. We might well abbreviate the word "micrometers" as "microns" and use the symbol "μm." (Note that we use the greek *mu* to represent millionths.) A table of common point thicknesses is as follows:

Inches	Micrometers	Inches	Micrometers
.001	25	.009	229
.002	51	.010	254
.003	76	.011	279
.004	102	.012	305
.005	127	.013	330
.006	152	.014	356
.007	178	.015	381
.008	203	.016	406

The above is only a partial table of micron thicknesses. In all cases we have rounded to the nearest whole number. To convert greater point thicknesses, simply multiply by 25.4 and round out to the nearest whole number as in the examples above.

Grammage Formula

If you do not have the grammage conversion chart handy, here is a formula that will work for every occasion. Consider these problems: What is the grammage of 65 lb cover stock? Also, 80 lb coated book? The formula is:

$$\frac{\text{Basis weight (lb)} \times 1406.5}{\text{Square inches in base size}}$$

Table 7-2.   Conversion chart showing common sizes in inches and their
equivalent in millimeters. This was accomplished by
multiplying inches by 25.4, then rounding out to the
nearest whole number.

Inches	Millimeters to tenth	Millimeters rounded
5½	139.7	140
6	152.4	152
7	177.8	178
8½	215.9	216
9	228.6	229
11	279.4	279
14	355.6	356
17	431.8	432
19	482.6	483
20	508.0	508
22	558.8	559
23	584.2	584
24	609.6	610
25	635.0	635
26	660.4	660
28	711.2	711
29	736.6	737
34	863.6	864
35	889.0	889
38	965.2	965
40	1016.0	1016
44	1117.6	1118
45	1143.0	1143
48	1219.2	1219
50	1270.0	1270

Basis weight size: cover is 20 × 26; book is 25 × 38.   Constant factor: 1406.5 (this factor is *constant*).   Substituting:

$$\frac{65 \times 1406.5}{20 \times 26} = 176$$

$$\frac{80 \times 1406.5}{25 \times 38} = 118$$

For your convenience we have included a table of inches to milli-meter conversions, Table 7-2.

Metric Temperature

Temperature is another factor that should be of interest. Our pres-ently used Fahrenheit scale will eventually go out with the foot, inch, and yard. In its place we shall talk about Celsius (formerly known as centigrade).

Figure 7-4 shows several comparisons. Water freezes and boils at 0° and 100° Celsius, respectively. These are easy numbers to remember—much easier than the Fahrenheit equivalents of 32° and 212°. Our body temperature is 37°C.

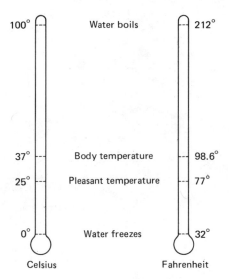

Figure 7-4. Comparative temperatures of both the old (Fahrenheit) and the new (Celsius) scales.

How would you like to take a *winter* vacation with a 25° temperature and soak up some sunshine in the Caribbean? That's fine if you're talking about 25° Celsius. If it's 25°F, you'll need an overcoat at the very least.

Here are the formulas for converting—a very easy task if you resort to your pocket calculator.

$$C = \tfrac{5}{9}(F - 32)$$

$$F = \tfrac{9}{5}C + 32$$

Now that you've read this simple chapter on metrics, don't hesitate to refer to it, and reread it from time to time. Your transition to metrication will be easier with each reading.

8

JOB LOT PAPER

Job lot paper represents a *secondary market* for the sale of printing papers. There are quite a few reasons why paper is classed as job lot, and we shall try to cover many of them; to mention every one is an impossibility.

The words "job lot" imply that paper in this category is imperfect, rejected paper that a mill refuses to sell to its customers. That happens to be true—job lot paper can be either imperfect or a reject—but it is only a small part of the story. On the other hand, in this secondary market the paper can be perfect, printable paper, suitable for four-color process printing!

Does the truth lie somewhere in between? Not so. This secondary market, commonly called job lot, is greatly misunderstood, which is the reason why this chapter is written. Please bear with us as we try to untangle the mystery.

The first, and perhaps more important, question to clarify is: why should there be a secondary market for paper? There is an adequate number of first-quality paper merchants who do an excellent job in the distribution and sale of fine-quality printing papers.

Let us turn to other industries that have the same problem, since we feel that by analogy the solution will be brought into sharper focus. The clothing industry is a good example because everyone buys the product. Let's start with men's suits.

Secondary Markets

In large metropolitan areas, newspapers and radio advertising extol the value of good buys in clothing at discount prices. Where do these good buys come from? How can large discount retailers offer these bargains? Part of the answer undoubtedly lies in volume retailing. Another large part is in volume buying, since these discount merchants have either very large or numerous outlets. Also, they make deals with manufacturers who are pinched for cash, and they pay promptly to get a better price.

Look at the manufacturers' side of the picture. Clothing is designed and produced in large volume with the hope of having a good selling season. Steady-volume manufacturing and purchase of large quantities of raw materials (cloth) mean lower unit costs. Everybody has competition, and for the most part their problems are the same.

Then comes adversity in the form of bad weather, stiff competition, economic considerations, and even credit problems. Isn't it good business to clean out inventory at a lower profit and convert frozen assets into cash? As consumers we should be glad that the manufacturers have this outlet—if they didn't, we would have to pay more money for our clothes.

Sweaters, knits, socks—consumers buy them all. What happens if something goes wrong with equipment (or people) and the result is a slight irregularity? The manufacturer has a reputation for top-notch merchandise and does not sell the product under his own name. Some outlets advertise this merchandise as irregulars at special prices—otherwise, it would represent a 100% loss. For many consumers the bargain is more important than a slight irregularity that no one can notice.

Cotton Rejects

What happens to cotton products, such as men's shirts or women's dresses? If there is just a slight irregularity, the product goes to one type of market. If it is too greatly defective, there is a *third* market—the *paper industry*!

Are you shocked? If so, look at your letterhead. It probably contains the cotton rejects we're talking about. . . .

By this time you are probably getting closer to the point—the fact that alternate solutions exist, thank goodness, before excess or defective merchandise goes into the scrap heap. *If this were not so, we would be paying higher prices for everything*, not to mention the gigantic solid waste disposal problem we would incur.

Finally, let's make a comparison with the automobile industry. In the United States, with a population of well over two hundred million people, the average yearly sale is approximately ten million new cars. But just as with calling job lot paper defective merchandise, that is only *part* of the story. There are many *used* cars sold every year, the secondary automobile market.

Many of the ten million car buyers, that is, *new* car buyers, are people who are trading in their autos after a year or more of use. How could those people buy new cars if they did not get a market allowance for their old ones? If there were no secondary market, people would hold their old cars longer, causing a serious effect on the production of new ones.

We now return to the paper industry, which has many of the problems of other manufacturers even though its primary raw material is wood. (As we have seen, of course, some papers require the addition of cotton fibers, and all papers have a great need for fillers and chemicals.)

Paper Below Mill Standard

If paper that has just been made is not up to mill standard for any reason, shall we dump it? Shall we put it back into the hopper and start the manufacturing process all over again? From an economic standpoint, it is cheaper to ship it out to the secondary market rather than tie up valuable storage space, or recycle it, or try any other disposal solution you can think of.

There is a definite need for a secondary market in paper, just as strong a need as that for a secondary market for automobiles. In evaluating the job lot market, I have asked pertinent questions and visited merchants. This research, coupled with my graphic arts experience of over three decades, has led to the conclusions outlined in the following discussion.

Job Lot Defined

The first question: *What is a job lot? Is it a mill reject? Mill overrun? The result of other valid reasons?*

A job lot may well be defined as a quantity of paper sold by a job lot merchant who buys the paper at a discount from the regular market price. Inasmuch as the lion's share is bought from paper mills, it is labeled "job lot" or "seconds" to distinguish the shipment from regular, first-line merchandise.

Read the definition again. Can you determine from the definition what the condition of the paper is? Of course not. The answers are many and varied. Furthermore, what about the second statement? If the job lot merchant doesn't get all his paper from the manufacturing mills, where else can he get it?

Customer Paper Disposal

Did you ever read an advertisement with a box number reply offering paper for sale? Were you ever in a situation where you for any reason found yourself with a lot of paper you could not use? Large publishers or other quantity paper consumers often are faced with this dilemma. Conditions change, generally owing to unforeseen circumstances.

Not too many years ago I was stuck with half a carload of 50-inch machine coated paper. It was sold to a job lot merchant for half the price I paid for it. This was mill-perfect paper, of course—yet it was eventually sold as job lot. Isn't it better to get 50% of your investment back than lose 100%? Other mitigating factors include trucking removal and storage costs.

Getting back to our initial remarks, job lot paper can be a mill reject. In fact, that is the most common reason for it. On the other hand, what constitutes a mill reject?

1. *Paper not up to mill standards.* A grade of paper calls for a certain shade of whiteness, tear strength, pick resistance, coating standard, bulk, opacity—even basis weight. Failure to meet these conditions, for any reason, may well be a cause for mill rejection.

What would the mill do with it? Recycle it? Throw it back into the stock chest and process it all over again? It is more economical from any standpoint to sell it at a discount and move it promptly off the premises.

Then comes the next question, who is going to buy it, and how shall it be used? We'll get to that later.

Mill Overrun

2. *Mill overrun.* This implies that the mill made more paper than the orders warranted. That, too, can be due to many and varied reasons. Someone may have made an error so that the paper was duplicated—perhaps by making two carloads of a certain size rather than one. Perhaps the size was 39 × 53—a size of paper I used to buy for many years! Believe it or not, the paper mechant ordered one carload too many when we decided to change the specifications. It would be a common practice for the job lot merchant to trim that lot and sell it as either 38 × 50 or 25 × 38. From the standpoint of economics, the merchant must have a sufficient discount to justify the handling, trimming, repacking—either in cartons or on skids—and the final shipment to the customer.

Let's face it—isn't it a great idea to have a job lot merchant around to take up the slack and get somebody out of trouble? (Aren't you glad that your old automobile has some resale value after you decide that it's time for a change?)

Side Runs

There is also a situation called a "side run." Let us say that a mill has a 135″ machine and has orders for a carload each of 35″ and 45″ rolls. Perhaps the orders are combined, or maybe they are processed individually. Whatever the reason, there is side or quantity excess of this mill-perfect paper. Since this paper will be sold at a discount, it is resold as a job lot.

Other Reasons

3. *Other reasons.* We couldn't possibly enumerate all the possibilities under this category, but again let me quote from my own experience.

A carload of paper, 50 lb offset size 38 X 50, was causing some difficulty. The mill representative came down and saw that the paper was two-sided: one side ran well; the backup linted badly. At his request, a skid was removed and another of his choosing was put on the press. Same results. Another skid was tried in his presence, and the trouble seemed to be uniformly the same. By mutual agreement the entire carload of 15 skids was rejected.

This lot obviously was sold to a job lot merchant. As for my problem, the mill offered to ship more paper in a few days. That was unsatisfactory from a time standpoint, since there was a delivery date involved. The mill representative was most apologetic but could do no better regarding the time element. I told him not to worry about it, that there was an alternate solution. A phone call to a job lot merchant solved the problem. In four hours' time we received four skids of 38 X 50 paper, which ran well and met the deadline. (See Figure 8-1.) The mill compensated the printer for lost press time, since this was a legitimate complaint.

Defective Cover Stock

Truth is said to be stranger than fiction. There was another instance involving a lot of coated cover that could not be used—even before it went on the press. As I accompanied the mill man to the printing plant, he was very emphatic about letting me know that only in very rare cases would the mill allow its paper to be rejected. His organization took great pride in the quality of its products and therefore it must be the fault of the printer.

When we entered the plant, the defective stock lay open for inspection. The mill man stared in amazement at the cover stock, the

Figure 8-1. A skid of paper is loaded onto a waiting truck for immediate delivery to a customer. (*Courtesy Cross Siclare/New York*).

like of which he had never seen.   Half of the paper was flat and uni-form.   The other half of the same sheet took a sudden dip, and the end curled back up to a point level with its opposite side. "How could this paper ever pass inspection?" he muttered in a tone of disbelief.   His terse comment, brief and to the point: "Pack it up and we'll take it out."

You are probably wondering what happens to this type of reject. That subject will be discussed later.

The Job Lot Merchant

The second query in this survey is: *What is the function of the job lot merchant in the graphic arts industry?*

Much of this question has already been answered in the previous examples.   Other questions will also have overlapping areas, but we'll try to offer different examples in each instance.

We have already observed the job lot merchant as an outlet for mill rejects, side runs, paper that was duplicated because of human error, paper liquidated by someone whose specifications had changed, or paper that was damaged in transit (see Figure 8-2). All of the paper had to be resold. The merchant bought his inventory below market value and passed the discount on to other customers.

Figure 8-2. A battered roll of paper from a printing plant is brought to the merchant for salvage. The roll can be either rewound after removal of the damaged layers, or it can be sheeted. (*Courtesy Cross Siclare/New York*).

Are you skeptical about a mill reject being resold? Perhaps the new buyer is a better craftsman who is smart enough to buy a lot of paper that is strictly an economy job lot for a light ink coverage job. Perhaps the final job calls for political handbills or small store promotions that require a very low price. (Even though you wouldn't ever drive that 10-year-old jalopy on the highway, that doesn't mean that someone of lower earning power can't utilize its cheap transportation.)

Those same promotional flyers, by the way, are often printed on one side only—ideal for that rejected carload that printed well on one side and linted on the other.

Sheeting from Rolls

The job lot merchant's role is also changing because the mills are sheeting less paper than they used to. This brings other roll problems to the fore. If a roll is not uniformly wound, it will cause trouble on a web press by having excessive web breaks. If the roll is "soft," that is, not wound tightly, it may have an uneven feed, causing still more web trouble. (See Figure 8-3.) That is another reason for rejection. The paper may well be perfect in all other respects, and is an ideal candidate for sheeting to a customer's specifications (see Figure 8-4.)

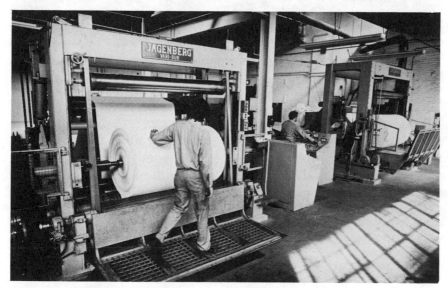

Figure 8-3. Rewinding rolls for proper tension and balance in preparation for web printing. (*Courtesy Cross Siclare/New York*).

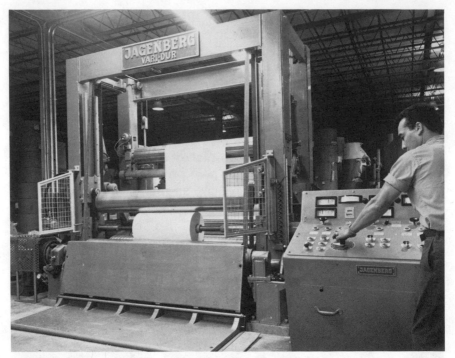

Figure 8-4. A roll of paper has been cut to a customer's specifications and is being rewound. (*Courtesy Case Paper Co.*)

Have you ever had occasion to use a nonstandard size? Why use 23 X 35 paper if you can utilize $19\frac{1}{2}$ X 34 *perfect paper* from your local job lot merchant? He can sheet from rolls if the quantity is large enough. Or you might just be lucky enough to be able to find a merchant with an odd size that cuts out with very little waste. You only pay for what you get. (See Figure 8-5.)

These are but a handful of reasons for the existence of a secondary paper market.

Secondary Outlets

The third question: *Why do paper mills sell to job lot paper merchants? What do they sell?*

Figure 8-5. Guillotine-trimming a ream of paper. (*Courtesy Cross Siclare/New York*)

A paper mill sells to job lot merchants as a secondary outlet for paper that does not meet the mill's rigid standards. If the paper is not the exact shade it was supposed to be, that is reason for rejection. It must be moved out promptly because it takes up valuable storage space and would constitute undesirable inventory. Granted this rejected paper is sold at a discount—that beats taking a 100% loss. The mill, too, has a disposal problem—that costs money also. Therefore it goes to the job lot market with the stipulation that it be sold as a job lot.

Buyer Testing

From the buyer's standpoint, the purchase of this paper is not a 100% gamble. Why? Simply because the job lot merchant has a policy of tagging the paper with an identification number, and takes samples for his files. (See Figure 8-6.) When a customer requests a sample of the paper for inspection, it is readily available. The buyer may then make some of his own tests: caliper, inspection of the shade, simple pick tests, groundwood content, tearing the sheet at right angles, studying the formation, and other evaluations. All of these can be done quickly by the experienced buyer.

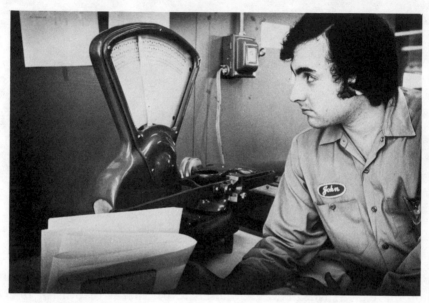

Figure 8-6. Checking the basis weight of a paper sample taken from an incoming mill lot. (*Courtesy Cross Siclare/New York*)

It is not uncommon for a mill to change the specifications for particular grades—generally upgrading. When that is done, old inventory is liquidated to the secondary market. The same reasoning holds for discontinued grades. How about excess inventory when economic conditions slow down? This is another way of evening out the peaks and valleys of supply and demand. Incidentally, when the demand for paper is strong, the mill inventory is generally low, and paper is moving out as fast as it is manufactured. The job lot merchant feels the tightening of the market, and his sources become less plentiful.

Of course, there are still the other mill defects we have indicated before, not to mention odd lot sizes that seem to crop up everywhere in paper manufacture, both in rolls and sheets.

Is the Paper Fit to Print

The fourth question: *Does the job lot merchant sell the paper as "fit to print," or is the buyer taking a gamble?*

As far as the job lot merchant is concerned, he is selling printable paper, and if the customer finds the paper unsatisfactory, it is returnable for full credit. By saying "full credit," we mean that the printer must determine very quickly that the paper is unacceptable.

Let us assume that a skid of paper is loaded onto the press, and the pressman finds he has to "fight" the paper. It may be wavy; have tight edges because of changes in moisture content (due to changes in relative humidity); feed improperly; lint; pick; have clay lumps, fiber bundles, slime holes; crease on press; or be defective for many other reasons. These defects should be discovered after running a small amount of paper, and the printer should advise the paper merchant of his dissatisfaction. Furthermore, the paper should be removed from the press quickly and not after spoiling several thousand sheets. The trade custom is only to take back paper that has not been cut, printed, or otherwise rendered unsuitable for resale.

Complaints

Since the printer or other customer has purchased job lot paper, there can be no claims for lost press time. The merchant will, however, take back the unsuitable paper and issue a credit upon its return. If this were first-quality paper, on the other hand, and if the same complaints were made, the paper merchant who sold the paper would send his representative down to the plant to confirm the paper defects, if any. In addition, the mill representative often appears for the same reason.

At this point we must bring up other factors regarding the sale of paper by the job lot merchant. There can be no question that there is more risk in purchasing job lot paper than when buying mill-perfect stock. As for the gamble in making the purchase, *this should be minimized*. How? By proper exchange of information between buyer and seller.

Two-Way Communication

Job lot paper buying is not for the novice. The buyer should confide in the merchant, advising of the type of job to be run, number of colors to be printed, whether the ink coverage is heavy or light, whether there are many halftones or none at all. In turn, the salesperson should be honest with the buyer and advise whether or not the paper is suitable for his particular need! Of course, there is a certain amount of risk, we repeat, but it can be minimized by proper communication on both sides.

Other factors that will affect the paper are weather and temperature, relative humidity, packing, handling. Paper should have sufficient time to adjust to its new surroundings in the printing plant and remain sealed until ready for use.

Frostbite

Getting back to my own experience, I recall ordering a carton of cover stock from my regular fine-paper distributor. It was a normally cold day in February, and the paper was opened almost immediately for the usual rush job. This first-quality paper was frozen solid in the center, and the outside edges curled upwards. Unquestionably the paper was smooth and even when it left the mill. In the jobber's warehouse, unheated, it succumbed to weather conditions and never thawed out properly.

There are endless arguments as to why paper will not print properly. Light-weight paper and dry conditions are fertile breeding grounds for static electricity. In these situations the feeding of paper can be a nightmare for a pressman. All we can suggest is that it be replaced as unsuitable, if no better answer can be found.

On the other hand, the pressman is not necessarily blameless. A good craftsman can resort to many tricks of his trade to overcome difficulties. A poor printer will complain at the first opportunity, blaming everyone and everything for his own deficiencies. This is true in every field of endeavor.

Merchant Sheeting

The fifth question: *Many job lot merchants carry sheeting equipment. Is this necessary, or optional?*

The larger job lot merchants feel that converting from rolls to sheets is an important part of the business. Paper mills are doing less sheeting where possible, since it is strictly a finishing operation. Furthermore, it adds to versatility and is an additional service to the buyer. (See Figure 8-7.)

Figure 8-7. Skid of paper, double-tiered, with ream markers. (*Courtesy Cross Siclare/New York*)

Rolls and Half Rolls

Slitting rolls and rewinding is another service that comes under finishing operations. We have had occasion where we needed 35″ and $17\frac{1}{2}$″ rolls to complete an order. For example, running a 40-page catalog, $8\frac{1}{2} \times 11$ on a web press using 70 lb coated stock meant using $2\frac{1}{2}$ rolls per book. This type of press has a fixed cutoff from $22\frac{1}{2}$ to $23\frac{1}{2}$ inches, depending on web design. For example:

$$\begin{array}{r} 35 \quad \times 23 \\ 8\frac{1}{2} \times 11 \\ \hline 4 \quad \times \ 2 = 8 \text{ pages on one side of a web,} \end{array}$$
$$\text{totaling 16 pages per signature}$$

The second signature used $1\frac{1}{2}$ webs, or one 35-inch roll and one $17\frac{1}{2}$″ roll. The half roll yields 8 pages (4 on each side) and com-

Figure 8-8. A roll of paper, slit to customer specifications, wrapped and ready for delivery. (*Courtesy Cross Siclare/New York*)

bines with the full roll to make up a 24-page signature, press-folded on the web. In the binding operation, both the 24-page and the 16-page signatures combined to form the 40-page catalog.

If you are wondering why this same type of service cannot be rendered by the paper mill, the answer is that it can—provided that you order a carload of paper at one time. The above order only totaled about 13,000 lb. (See Figure 8-8.)

Since the tendency seems to be for mills to do less sheeting, we know of smart paper salesmen who have speeded up deliveries by buying perfect paper in rolls and having it delivered to job lot merchants for conversion to special sheet sizes.

When to Buy a Job Lot

When should the buyer purchase a job lot, and when should he not do so? This is the sixth question, and again it has been partially answered in other discussions.

The quick answer for when to buy, of course, is to save money. The next answer for a printer may well be that if he does not buy his paper cheaper, he cannot compete and will lose many jobs. This opens up a large number of questions, but we must again repeat that buying a job lot offers much more risk. Unfortunately a buyer cannot always get the full story of why a lot of paper has been siphoned off to the job lot market.

Quick Availability

Time is always an important element in a printing job. In most cases there are delays all along the line in preparation of copy, artwork, changes in specifications, delay in manufacturing a product, or whatever. In the meantime, the deadline for the printed piece keeps getting closer, and by the time the printer gets the copy, he has to close the gap somewhere. This delay is further aggravated because the quantity of stock is unknown owing to the number of pages being flexible and the number of copies needed not being finally determined. The job lot merchant has the advantage of being able to make quick delivery from stock, or sheeting from rolls. An important plus factor for the job lot merchant is the ability to deliver a nonstandard sheet size, which means less paper waste for the printer. For example, a $19\frac{1}{2}$ × 32-inch sheet is less costly than a standard 23 × 35.

Using 60 lb basis stock:

$$23 \quad \times 35 = 102 \text{ lb per M sheets}$$

$$19\frac{1}{2} \times 32 = \quad 79 \text{ lb per M sheets}$$

The differential represents a saving of 23 lb per thousand sheets. If 10,000 sheets are required for the job, the saving is 230 lb. Multiplied by the cost per pound, such as 40¢, this means a saving of $92.00 on a small order of paper.

When Not to Buy a Job Lot

When should a buyer *not* buy a job lot? If the budget permits, and first-quality paper is readily available, there is no reason for unnecessary gambles. If the printed piece calls for heavy ink coverage, especially on coated stock, why take a chance? If top quality is of prime importance . . . need we say more?

We stated earlier that there should be better communication between buyer and seller of job lot paper. The buyer should not take unnecessary risks, nor should the seller fail to caution the buyer if he feels the lot of paper to be bought is questionable for the job.

Job Lot Paper Information

Question seven: *Does the job lot paper merchant know the reason why paper is sold by the mill?* Generally speaking, the merchant has a good idea why paper is sold to him, but not always. There can be some piecing together of information by knowing the mill, its products, and other experience. If further information is needed, the merchant can call the mill and ask additional questions.

On the other hand, we have indicated some of the reasons, such as excess inventory, paper not conforming to rigid mill standards, old shades, discontinued lines, side runs, or outright rejects because of defects.

In this competitive world, a progressive job lot merchant who looks ahead, utilizes modern sheeting and handling equipment, and keeps up with the latest changes in the paper situation, will usually fare better than his counterpart who is satisfied with the "status quo" of simply buying and selling limited lines. (See Figure 8-9.)

One of the job lot merchants I contacted had a paper-testing office, which tested different lots for various characteristics. (See Figure

Figure 8-9. Press-cut paper, packed in cartons, ready for shipment. (*Courtesy Case Paper Co.*)

8-10.) This merchant also has gone into the first-quality paper business, buying paper in rolls, sheeting various sizes, and offering full mill guarantees on his paper. Since he also has sheeting and rewinding equipment, his service is that much more valuable.

No paper merchant can be all things to all people. The paper buyer must have several sources at his disposal if he purchases many types of paper. However, the knowledge of where to get what he needs, the right quality at the right price, separates the professional from the amateur.

We could go on endlessly, but enough has been said, we think, to clarify the meaning of the job lot market. One final example will show that no one has all the answers.

Cast Coated Job Lot

A buyer bought a lot of *cast coated* job lot paper, coated on both sides. The paper ran very well on its first side; when completed, it was turned over and fed back into the press. The second side was so

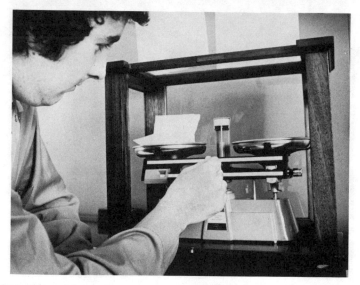

Figure 8-10. Determining moisture content on a humidity scale. (*Courtesy Cross Siclare/ New York*)

impossible to run because of picking and bad feeding that the printer could not continue. This is very expensive paper even in the secondary category. The paper could not be returned because it was printed. The loss of press time was an additional loss. Replacing the paper with another order meant more time wasted. There is no recourse in such situations. Had the paper been bought as first-line merchandise, it would have represented a legitimate mill complaint.

The final market for unsuitable stock is not necessarily the wastepaper dealer—that is the *final* answer. Shirt manufacturers and other industries can use the paper as stuffers and linings, and for a host of other purposes. Blank tablet paper and memo pads, not printed, might represent other third-market usage, like the selling of "unsalable" cotton fabrics to the paper industry.

"Hello? Guinness Book of Records? What's the record for the most job lot paper made during a shift?"

Reprinted from *Pulp and Paper Magazine*, January 1978. Cartoon by Ron Lewis.

9
RECYCLING AND ECOLOGY

Recycling and *ecology* are predominant words in our society. As a nation, the United States has 6% of the world's population, yet uses 33% of the world's energy and resources. This enviable living standard is now taking its toll, straining our natural resources and forcing an evaluation of their present and future state.

Per Capita Consumption

In the paper industry, the paramount natural resource is wood fiber. Fortunately this is a renewable resource. Unfortunately we are faced with a situation where it is now possible to consume more trees than regrowth will allow. Our per capita consumption of paper and paper products has reached approximately 650 lb per year, and the end is nowhere in sight.

Our high living standard has brought wasteful practices. We consume newspapers and other publications in enormous quantities and discard them just as easily. Sharp marketing practice has been to package almost every conceivable product in a paper container, with food packaging increasing at an unprecedented rate. Just as with our daily newspaper, we take our food from the package and discard the paper and plastic packaging, tossing it into our garbage cans.

Now we have created new problems. Garbage disposal requires energy in a removal process. Garbage dumps are unsightly and unsanitary, nor are there endless areas for dumping. Burning garbage causes a huge air pollution problem. Using the garbage as landfill is also costly, in land area, transportation, and sanitary-landfill methods.

Private industry is also a large polluter in the form of waste disposal and dumping of effluent material into lakes, rivers, and other areas. The solution to these problems—if there is a solution—is the subject of this chapter.

*   *   *   *

Source of Wood Fiber

Starting at the beginning, let us look at the source of wood fiber, and see where we are and where we might be headed.

Near the beginning of this book, we indicated, in Figure 1-1, that the forest products industry holds only 14% of the 500 million acres of woodlands in the United States. Private ownership accounts for 59% of the woodlands, whereas our national forests represent 18%.

In Figure 1-2 we showed that the forest products industry harvests 26% of the timber used. Our national forests harvest 16%, while private ownership, with 59% of the holdings, accounts for 51% of the harvesting.

Interpreting these statistics, we note that the forest products industry has secured the maximum yield per acre. This is quite normal, since timber is its primary product. On the other hand, our national parks have the primary function of being available for recreation and natural beauty, so why harvest public lands?

The answer is that trees are living organisms and, just like other forms of life, have a limited life span. If left alone, one-fifth of them will succumb to such natural hazards as fire, insect infestation, or blowdown. In the United States, we cannot afford this loss while trying to maintain our high living standards. Furthermore, an area of fallen trees is unpleasant to both human and wild life, besides, among other disadvantages, being a fire hazard.

Forest Control

Logically, selective harvesting and building access roads to the forest interior will serve many useful purposes. These roads will enable the Forest Service to exercise better control of wildfire, as well as make more of our public lands accessible for recreation. One way to combat insect devastation would be premature harvesting. Experience has shown that clearcutting planned areas is the most feasible answer, since it also allows better control. Replanting trees of a superior strain also makes sense. The funds for these operations can come from the sale of harvested timber in our public forests.

At this writing, our serious conservationists have succeeded in restraining timber harvesting in the Monongahela National Forest in West Virginia, as well as the Tongass National Forest in Alaska. With demand increasing constantly, where will we obtain the additional resources?

Tree Farm

The forest product companies are exercising good forest management in harvesting and new planting, as mentioned earlier. This is not enough, especially in view of the limited acreage under their control. A plus factor is their program of working with private owners in a tree farm system. Good silvicultural practices are emphasized in order to increase the private yield, which, in turn, is sold to the forest products industry.

Another plus is the utilization of more of the wood in the forest. On the one hand, whole-tree chipping in the forest means using branches as well as the more desirable tree trunks. Also, sawdust, which used to be a total waste, is utilized as fuel and pulpwood, and in other manufactured products.

Bark

Not long ago, wood bark was burned in wigwam burners in an endless fire as a means of its disposal. Today, the same bark is used as a mulch, in fertilizer, and also as fuel in the papermaking process to generate energy and steam. In fact, there is such a turnabout that in some cases lumber mills are baling bark for sale to papermakers.

In Figure 1-10 we observed the huge increase in the use of wood residue from sawmills. This residue is chipped at the source and shipped to paper mills. It has become an important factor in pulpwood procurement. And, as we saw in Figure 1-4, pulpwood constitutes less than 32% of the total timber harvest.

Additional Pulp Sources

Finally, where shall we procure more wood pulp? We can gaze longingly at our neighbor to the north as well as Alaska. In both cases there is a huge transportation problem, the most important aspect of which is the shipping cost. Of course, the wood can be converted to chips at or near their source. Also, instead of blowing the chips into a waiting truck, it makes more sense to bale them, which offers the added advantage of compressing the wood into a smaller area for transportation purposes. Moreover, since some of the moisture is squeezed out in the process, the bales can remain in storage longer than an open chip pile.

Realistically, by virtue of there being a colder climate up north, trees grow at a much slower rate there than they do in the United States. In addition, much of the Canadian forest is presently inaccessible because it lies in undeveloped territory. In order to exploit this hidden resource, there must be economic justification in the form of higher timber values. This means increased cost to the consumer—always an unpopular and undesirable solution.

Importing wood fiber is another possibility. We do have imports, but we also have exports. The latest available statistics from the U.S. Department of Commerce show that we import slightly more than we export, but only to a small degree.

Finally, an expanding population with a constantly rising living standard increases the need for pulpwood and timber for other uses (e.g., building homes, furniture, industrial construction, and the like). By the same token, some of the forest may be converted into farmland to grow more food.

Recycling Defined

The best answer to obtaining more wood fiber is to reuse paper and boxboard. This is the *recycling process—reclaiming the product after it has served its initial purpose and putting it back into the main-stream in another form.* Of course it must be treated in several ways, such as deinking, bleaching, removing additives. The fiber can then be utilized not only for reuse in printing papers, but also in such household necessities as toilet tissue, paper towels, napkins, box-board, chipboard, and an infinite number of other paper products.

Solid Waste Problem

The other side of the picture is the need to reduce the solid waste disposal problem. Municipal trash contains from 40% to 60% news-paper and other paper products that could be profitably utilized in a recycling program. The collection of this material is costly to the consumer in the form of local taxes or, in some areas, local pickup charges. We are badly in need of an educational program to stimulate collection of paper and paper products.

Many organizations find the collection of newspapers an excellent source of revenue. On the other hand, when paper production is below normal owing to decreased demand, the value of waste paper tumbles to the point where the scrap dealer finds it unprofitable to pick it up. This may seem contradictory to what we are saying, so let's put it another way.

Suppose we had a planned program whereby the local authorities made it unlawful to place old newspapers and boxboard in a container with other household garbage. Automatically, 50% of the pickup for garbage disposal would be separated as a useful, recoverable commodity. It could be picked up, let us say, once each week by a separate truck that followed the regular garbage truck. In some outlying areas, once per month might be more feasible, but that could be determined locally.

Newspaper Collection

The newspapers could either be tied with string or put in used shopping bags and placed alongside the household garbage container. For recycling purposes, use of a shopping bag is better than string tying because the string itself is a contaminant. It is better *not* to use a plastic disposal bag because it is also a contaminant and might be better used for other refuse.

Another way of collecting the old paper is to have a central collection point established by a local church, Boy Scouts, or other groups. The revenue derived from this sort of enterprise is important from a fund-raising standpoint if enough people cooperate in the plan. If an adequate amount of tonnage is collected, the local waste paper dealer (who is listed in the yellow pages of the telephone directory) will be glad to send a pick-up truck and pay for the privilege of hauling it away.

It is true that there will always be a supply and demand situation to alter the value of the collection. However, if it were unlawful to throw away old paper indiscriminately, there would be a large upsurge in the amount of waste paper available. This steady source of supply, in turn, would assure paper mills, boxboard plants, and other users of waste paper that they could depend on waste paper dealers to meet their requirements. The end result could be a most healthy one for the entire nation—reusing our waste products more efficiently and lessening the solid waste removal problem.

Other Paper Waste Sources

Of course there are many other sources of waste paper besides the household. Large offices and business establishments of all kinds are throwing every conceivable type of paper into the trash collection pile. It can be most effectively utilized if placed in special recepta-cles for the purpose.

Office waste, including the ever growing printed output from com-puter installations, is of a much higher grade than newsprint, and therefore would command a better price from the salvage dealer. Once again, it must be collected in separate receptacles and bundled together or baled for easy removal. The highest grade of waste paper is the kind that is chemically free of groundwood. Most office sta-tionery falls into this category. Local offices should seek an incen-tive to get employees to be careful in separating waste into appropri-ate, individual receptacles. One way might be to declare a cash divi-dend from the year's receipts in time for end-of-the-year shopping. Other ideas might be to provide a special slush fund from which re-tiring employees could receive a gift, or which could be used for some other special occasion. There is no end to creative thinking—provided there is an incentive.

Figure 9-1. Sorting and grading paper. Maintaining quality control standards is an impor-tant job of the paper stock processor. (*Courtesy National Association of Recycling Industries*)

Contaminants

Regardless of how careful people are, there are always some contaminants mixed in with the paper. They might be paper clips, staples, string, or just anything at all. These items have to be sorted out before the waste can be utilized. Figure 9-1 is an example of sorting and grading paper by paper stock processors.

In Figure 9-2, after being sorted and graded the paper stock is baled according to mill specifications and is ready for shipment.

Figure 9-2. Baling the cleaned, graded paper stock in weights and sizes according to the specifications of the paper mill. (*Courtesy National Association of Recycling Industries*)

When the waste stock is received at the manufacturing plant, it will again go through a careful inspection to be sure that only fibrous material is being processed. In Figure 9-3 the material is put through a

Figure 9-3. Beating and cleaning, the first step in the manufacturer's recycling process Here the fibers are bathed over and over again to remove any foreign matter. (*Courtesy National Association of Recycling Industries*)

beating and cleaning process to remove any unwanted matter that may be lingering in the waste paper.

The recycled furnish is then filtered to a uniform size by pumping the fibers through a series of large screens. After thorough cleaning, sorting, and screening, the reprocessed fibers are then ready for their next journey, as shown in Figure 9-4. These fibers may be used in making boxboard, in newsprint, or mixed with virgin fiber for fine papermaking.

In Figure 9-5 a finished roll from a paperboard mill is shown, containing a high percentage of recycled fibers. As indicated in the illustration, these rolls will be shipped to converting plants for use in some of the many consumer products.

Need for Legislative Incentives

Despite the serious need for recycling our resources, our legislators, by failing to add incentives to encourage the use of waste materials, are not cooperating. One very important idea is high freight rates, which must be added to the price of the finished recycled product. In turn, the recycling mills hesitate to purchase higher-cost fiber when they can procure virgin fiber for a lower cost.

The entire world is in an energy crisis, and it takes more energy to process virgin fiber than it does to recycle secondary fiber. The whole picture is so overwhelmingly in favor of recycling that our government must take immediate steps to pass legislation and enact other incentives to step up the recycling pace.

Figure 9-4. Screening is the next step in the recycling process. The material is filtered to a uniform size by pumping the fibers through a series of huge screens. After cleaning, sorting, and screening, the fibers are ready to be formed into sheets of paper. (*Courtesy National Association of Recycling Industries*)

Figure 9-5. A finished roll, the final product of the paperboard mill. From here, rolls are shipped to converters and other manufacturers, who will convert them into consumer products. (*Courtesy National Association of Recycling Industries*)

The next phase of the recycling program is concerned with what to do with the paper waste that has already bypassed any separate collection system and is just plain garbage. This, unfortunately, is the largest part of the problem. Before going into that, let us quote some statistics from the booklet *Waste Paper Recycling*, published (and copyrighted) in 1975 by the American Paper Institute's Paper Stock Conservation Committee.

Waste Paper Statistics

During World War II, paper recycling was considerably higher than it is today, reaching a peak of 35.3% in 1944. While both paper usage and waste paper recycling have increased since that time, the *percentage* of paper recycled declined steadily until 1972. In 1974, for example, the United States consumed 65,700,000 tons of paper and paperboard and recycled 14,200,000 tons. Since the recycling figure represents only 22% of total consumption, what happened to the rest of the paper?

The American Paper Institute estimates that approximately 13,200,000 tons remained in permanent use in such forms as books and building materials, with some of this also disposed of as tissue products and fireplace fuel. An additional 1,300,000 tons were exported. What happened to the remaining 37,000,000 tons? Obviously they went into solid waste disposal.

Teamwork

Some municipalities are experimenting with solid waste problems in other than landfill operations. For example, as reported in the

Figure 9-6. Groveton Papers' former barking room now contains the dual-chamber incinerator used to dispose of both mill wastes and town refuse. (*Courtesy Paper Trade Journal*)

Paper Trade Journal of April 1, 1976, the town of Northumberland, New Hampshire, and Groveton Papers Co. have teamed up to incinerate the mill's combustible trash. One day per week the town's garbage is also burned in this plan, with a resulting production of 7,500 lb of 125-lb steam per hour. This has the dual effect of lowering the mill's energy consumption while simultaneously alleviating the garbage disposal problem. (See Figures 9-6 and 9-7.)

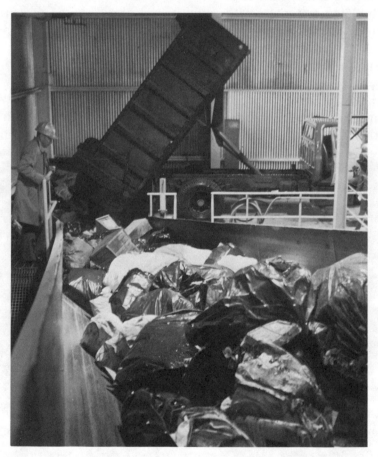

Figure 9-7. Refuse from the town of Northumberland, N.H., is dumped directly onto the incinerator feed conveyor at the Groveton Papers mill. (*Courtesy Paper Trade Journal*)

Similar plans for extracting energy from garbage are either in the planning stage or in actual practice in some other areas. This effort should be speeded up for the good of all concerned. Also being planned is extraction of wood fiber from the municipal collection effort, in addition to conversion of garbage to energy, thereby lessening both the volume and the tonnage of solid waste.

Referring again to Groveton Papers Co., it is interesting to note that the recent change of securing pulpwood from chips right in the forest left the company with an unneeded debarker as well as other space as a result of the changing technology.

Sanitary Landfill

Assuming that all paper fiber recovery efforts have been exhausted, the last stop is now the burial plot or sanitary landfill. Contrary to some popular beliefs, this is not a fancy name for a garbage dump. Solid waste is compacted into the smallest possible volume and hauled to a landfill area which is what the name indicates. The next step is to cover the waste with earth so that it will not be a breeding ground for rodents or scavengers.

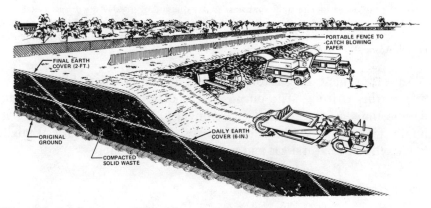

Figure 9-8. Area method. The bulldozer spreads and compacts solid wastes. The scraper (foreground) is used to haul the cover material at the end of the day's operations. Note the portable fence that catches any blowing debris. This is used with any landfill method. (*Courtesy Environmental Protection Agency*)

Designating an area for landfill is an engineering project. The geological features of the area are considered, since there will be a certain amount of settling, especially during the first two years. The nature of the soil, amount of moisture, compactness of the solid waste—all have a bearing on the effectiveness of the project. These landfill areas will then be ideal for such recreational uses as golf courses, ball fields, botanical gardens, and parks. We are indebted to the Environmental Protection Agency for the diagrams in Figures 9-8 and 9-9, which you may find of interest.

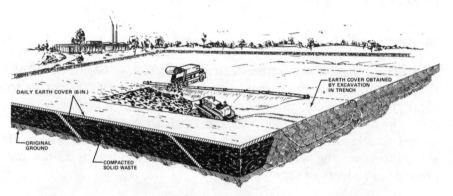

Figure 9-9. Trench method. The waste collection truck deposits its load into the trench, where the bulldozer spreads and compacts it. At the end of the day the dragline excavates soil from the future trench; this soil is used as the daily cover material. Trenches can also be excavated with a front-end loader, bulldozer, or scraper. (*Courtesy Environmental Protection Agency*)

An experiment in California regarding sanitary landfills is under way at this writing. The purpose is to extract methane gas from decomposing waste, recover it economically, then improve it for use in homes and industry. After treatment to improve its quality, it might be mixed with natural gas and piped to the consumer.

Other Recycling at the Mill

Getting back to our recycled fiber, there are other sources that we have not yet mentioned. One source is the paper mill itself. When a web of paper breaks in the manufacturing process, the assembly procedure stops. The wet end of the machine is producing an endless amount of good paper, but instead of there being a continuous web, a tremendous jam-up occurs, where paper, not fully dried, has broken from its web and is piling up at an astonishing rate. When this happens, mill personnel quickly assemble at the break and physically push the paper away from the machine. At the same time, other people quickly start a new web by breaking off the piled-up paper. If the roll at the winding end is not complete, the paper will be spliced and the winding process continued. Meanwhile, the paper waste, called "broke," is baled up and reused in the papermaking process, rather than being dumped into the solid waste stream.

Figure 9-10. A 110-inch trimmer, tape-operated for accuracy, cutting waste on its way to a conveyor for baling. (*Courtesy Case Paper Co.*)

Trim Waste

Another important source of recycled fiber is waste trimming at paper converters and printing plants, as well as boxboard manufacturing plants. Paper is cut to a required size, and the edge trim is waste. In Figure 9-10, a "fisheye" lens shows some of the edge trimmings being discarded from the cutter and sent on their way to a conveyor. In Figure 9-11 the trimmed edgings are discarded onto a conveyor. From here the waste travels to the baling room, where the material is bundled and stacked, awaiting removal by a waste paper dealer.

Figure 9-11. Straight photo view of the same 110-inch cutter sheeting paper to a customer's specifications. The waste trimmings are discarded to the conveyer belt, which transports them to the baling room for salvage and recycling. (*Courtesy Case Paper Co.*)

We now turn our attention to how the paper mills utilize recycled paper.

100% Recycling of Newsprint

In newsprint, Garden State Paper Company is the outstanding exception. This company makes newsprint exclusively from old newsprint—100% recycling. Much of the newsprint used in the United States is produced in Canada. However, Garden State alone accounts for 10% of all the newsprint manufactured in the United States.

Industrial paper packaging, boxboard, tissue, towels, and napkins all use a considerable amount of recycled fiber. In the fine-printing-paper field the percentage is unfortunately not as great.

Bergstrom Primer on Recycling

One of the most notable fine paper mills using recycled paper is the Bergstrom Paper Company. This company utilizes it to such a great extent that, with their permission, we have decided to make use of the description given in *A primer on how Bergstrom makes recycled paper*.

Paper is made from paper in two basic stages—fiber regeneration (pulping) and papermaking. The first stage essentially is a purification process in which reusable fibers are deinked, bleached, and cleaned through a series of precisely controlled mechanical, hydraulic, and chemical treatments, which get the pulp ready to become paper again. The following is a summary of the basic phases in Bergstrom's fiber recovery process.

Stage One—Fiber Recovery

1. *Raw Materials.* Most of Bergstrom's secondary fiber comes from dealers in major U.S. cities, with smaller amounts shipped from practically anywhere in the country.

Of the 46 standard grades of reusable paper available, the firm uses

17, which are suitable for recycling into papers used in commercial printing, business, publishing, and the graphic arts. The grades translate into three main categories of stock: book papers (about half-and-half groundwood and groundwood-free), ledger, and kraft. Typically, these include magazines, tabulating cards, computer print-out stock, office ledgers, certain high-grade cartons, business forms, and trim and cuttings from a variety of printers, including book manufacturers.

Though these papers have been carefully sorted by suppliers, they are reinspected at the Bergstrom mills to eliminate unacceptable materials.

2. *Pulping.* In the first phase, a conveyor system delivers the waste paper to a hydrapulper, a large vessel in which a solution of hot water, caustic, ink dispersants, detergents, and steam diffuses through the mix. Temperatures run 180°–200°F (81°–93°C), with chemical concentration varying according to the fiber being treated and the nature of ink dispersion on it. The hydrapulper's mixing action, much like that of a kitchen blender, reduces the contents to a slurried pulp. The stock is pumped to blending chests, where it is diluted further with hot water and chemicals.

After these phases begins the thorough round of washing, cleaning, bleaching, and screening necessary to remove the ink and other undesired materials, and yield clean, bright pulp. (See Figure 9-12.)

3. *Washing and Filtering.* Stock from the blending chests is pumped to a large drum filter, where it is washed and filtered and chemicals from the previous process are removed.

4. *Spin Cleaning.* Next the stock is routed to large centrifiers, which spin it to create centrifugal forces that remove staples, pins, paper clips and similar heavier-than-fiber objects.

5. *Vibratory Screening.* From the centrifiers, the acceptable stock passes over a series of vibratory screens, which remove wet-strength chips, bundles, plastic particles, and other rejectable materials. (See Figure 9-13.)

6. *Vacuum Filtering.* Stock refined by screening moves to vacuum filters, which recover heat and chemicals introduced thus far. The liquid is recirculated to the hydrapulping phase for further use.

7. *Bleaching.* Bergstrom papers get their whiteness from the company's three-phase bleaching process.

Washed pulp, held in a storage chest, is pumped to the first phase, the chlorination tower, where chlorine gas is introduced. The gas reacts with the woody fibers' natural-brownish-colored constituents. After chlorination, the pulp is washed and vacuum-screened on a drum to remove chlorinated compounds.

Figure 9-12. Making paper from paper is basically a purification process in which fibrous materials are separated from nonfibrous—ink, clay, and sizing for the most part—through precisely controlled mechanical, hydraulic, and chemical treatment. During one stage of the process, side hill washing and screening, the nearly recovered fibers in pulp form resemble cottage cheese.   On the average, 700 tons of finished paper per day are produced by the company's mills. (*Courtesy Bergstrom Paper Co.*)

Figure 9-13. Screen for removing plastics and other nonfibrous material from recovered paper fiber. (*Courtesy Black Clawson Co.*)

In the second phase of bleaching, the pulp is treated with caustic soda and sodium hypochlorite, drained, and washed again before going to the third phase, where hypochlorite is added a second time.

At the end of the bleaching process, the pulp is again washed and diluted to a thin slurry. Bleaching compounds are recovered for reuse.

8. *Screening and Cleaning.* From the bleachery the stock is diluted to pulp slurry and passed through the two stages of screens that reject undesired materials and fibers too large to pass through minute openings. Then come four stages of centricleaners, all cross-linked, whereby each stage sends its accepts to the stage ahead and its rejects to the previous stage.

9. *Reverse Centrifugal Cleaning.* While the previous centrifugal cleaners removed heavier-than-fiber materials, the second battery of these cleaners reject lighter-than-fiber impurities. This highly successful cleaning process is patented by Bergstrom and available to other firms under a licensing arrangement.

10. *Final Washing and Storage.* Acceptable stock goes next to a huge washer ($11\frac{1}{2}$ feet in diameter, 20 feet long, weighing 31 tons), which provides final washing and thickening of the pulp. An auger feeds the high-density pump, which sends the stock from the washer to either of two storage towers, which have a combined capacity of 450 tons. The stock at this point represents a 70–75% yield from the raw material that went into the hydrapulper initially. Gone are the ink, starches, plastics, pigments, and all other undesirables. (See Figure 9-14.)

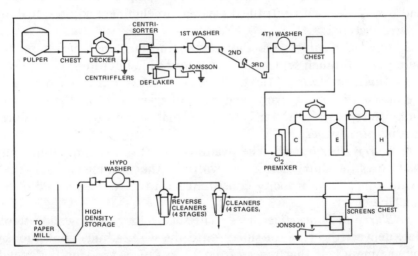

Figure 9-14. This simplified schematic of Bergstrom's deinking plant in Neenah shows the many carefully controlled phases that produce fine recycled fibers for making many kinds of papers. The company has a similar operation at its Moraine Mill in West Carrollton, Ohio. (*Courtesy Bergstrom Paper Co.*)

Stage Two—Making of Paper

Bergstrom's fourdrinier-type paper machines are highly automated to take fiber slurry at one end and deliver a variety of high-quality printing and writing papers at the other. A brief description of the papermaking process follows.

Blending

The proportion of pulp flowing from the holding chests, through a refining stage, and to the papermaking machines is continuously metered, as is the quantity of various additives, such as titanium dioxide, clay, rosin size, and alum. Dyes can also enter the flow to create specified color. Once set, the blend remains constant.

The Papermaking Machine

1. *Centri Cleaning.* At the machine, the pulp is diluted with water and passed through centrifugal cleaners to eliminate any residual undesired materials.

2. *Final Screening.* On the way to the machine's headbox, the pulp passes through screens to remove possible fiber lumps.

3. *Additives Added.* Next, other additives—alum and filler clay—are injected into the "white water" used again to dilute the pulp to a milky slurry. White water is the fluid that is drained from the slurry as it becomes paper.

4. *Slurry Distributed.* The headbox (front of machine) uniformly distributes the slurry across the width of the machine and delivers it to the "slice" at a velocity consistent with the running speed of the machine.

5. *Slurry to Fourdrinier Wire.* The slice, a long, narrow, adjustable slot, delivers the flow of slurry onto the wire, a huge continuously moving mesh belt that ranges from 75 to 117 feet in length, depending on the Bergstrom machine used.

6. *Paper Web Formed.* The wire moves and shakes the slurry from side to side, interlocking the tiny fibers and improving the formation and uniformity of the finished paper. Excess white water drains through the wire mesh, leaving a closely woven web of paper. The wire travels over a series of table rolls, foils, and suction boxes, which help to remove additional water.

A dandy roll rotating atop the wire creates even sides to the paper web and improves the formation. It can also be fitted with an etched plate that, upon making contact with the paper, puts an impression or watermark symbol into the paper.

7. *Pressing.* From the wire mesh, the web of paper, about 30% dry, goes to the press section, where more water is extracted between rubber rollers and woven wool felt. This phase also smooths and compacts the paper. At this point the paper is 45% dry.

8. *First Drying.* Now the web of paper is free to leave the felt carrier on its own strength and enter the drying section, where remaining water is removed by evaporation as the paper passes over cylinders steam-heated to temperatures ranging from 125°–260°F (52°–127°C).

9. *Second Drying, Sizing, Final Drying.* From the first dryer, the paper is carried into the second dryer section for the evaporation of more moisture. From here it passes through the size press, where the web of paper is treated with a starch film, or pigments, to fill its pores according to specific printing requirements. The paper is then routed through the third dryer section, where it has become 95% dry.

10. *Surface Finishing.* The paper continues on through the calender stack of chilled steel rolls, which compact it to give a fine smooth surface finish. The more pressure applied, the glossier the surface of the sheet.

11. *Automatic Detection.* A computer monitoring system regulates basis weight and moisture content, and also scans for imperfections.

12. *Winding and Rewinding.* At the dry end of the machine, the finished paper is wound on a large spool, then transferred to a rewinder. There it is rewound to desired diameters, slit to specific roll widths, and inspected.

13. *Weighing and Wrapping.* Finally, the finished rolls are weighed (paper is usually sold by weight), marked, and wrapped in moisture-proof wrap for shipment to printers and publishers who print directly from rolls on web-fed presses. Some rolls are sent to the mills' converting operations, where they are cut into different-size sheets for use on sheet-fed printing presses.

This completes the two-stage description of fiber recovery and papermaking. Not only does Bergstrom recycle waste paper to make new paper, but throughout the deinking and papermaking process, water and chemical compounds are intercepted and recirculated for reuse.

Water Discharge

Water ultimately discharged from the mills is processed through the company's own on-site treatment facilities. Clays and other virtually inert solids are collected and used for land fill. Discharges to the environment are closely controlled and filtered to pollution abatement standards.

Note how paramount the recycling issue becomes. Not only do we reclaim fiber for use in new paper products, but we also utilize chemicals, fillers, and additives to every possible extent. Waste water from the papermaking process is reused again and again. This recycling is an important part of protecting the environment, keeping our waterways clean, and minimizing land and air pollution.

The paper industry has spent billions of dollars in environmental projects to comply with government standards. This capital expenditure is badly needed for both modernization and expansion of mill capacity.

Biological Oxygen Demand

In past years, paper mills drew water for papermaking from adjacent bodies of water and poured their effluent back into them. Organically, there is a certain amount of self-purifying done by the rivers and lakes as bacteria break down the discharged waste. A problem arose when the effluent was being pumped back into the water faster than nature could digest it. In other words, the effluent exceeded the biological oxygen demand, known as B.O.D.

Primary Treatment

All paper mills now use some sort of treatment process before discharging waste water and other impurities. Some mills chemically treat the water in a neutralization basin before sending it to the clarifiers in what is known as primary treatment. In this type of treatment, waste is pumped into the clarifier, and by a settling process the solids sink to the bottom leaving the liquids on top, as shown in Figure 9-15.

Figure 9-15. Primary treatment. Two 105-foot primary clarifiers at I-P's Ticonderoga mill. All waste water from the mill goes first to the clarifiers, where all settlable solids are removed. These solids are then returned to the mill, where they are dewatered and burned in the mill's boilers. (*Courtesy International Paper Co.*)

Secondary Treatment

The liquid is now pumped to large lagoons for secondary treatment. The natural self-cleaning process is enhanced by aeration, pumping oxygen into the water to speed up the cleaning process. Figure 9-16 shows another view of the treatment facility, while Figure 9-17 is self-explanatory.

Another form of ingenuity is presented by the Simpson Lee mill at

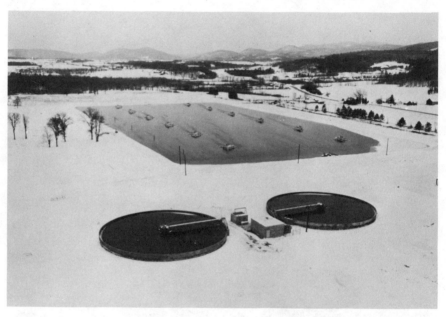

Figure 9-16. Secondary treatment. Secondary treatment for waste water is provided by this 67-million-gallon lagoon. Natural bacterial action in the lagoon removes 90% of the oxygen demand. Twelve floating aerators replenish the dissolved oxygen used up in the process, and also mix and cool the water. The treated water is then released to secondary clarifiers for final treatment. At full operation, the lagoon handles 21 million gallons of water a day. (*Courtesy International Paper Co.*)

Vicksburg, Michigan, which boasts of zero pollution. The mill effluent, after treatment, is spray-irrigated into fields adjoining the mill instead of being dumped into lakes and rivers.

Recycling is a vast enterprise, discussion of which can be almost endless. Our sole purpose in confining it to just one chapter is to acquaint the reader with the importance of the subject. In conclusion, here are some of the highlights of recycling and its resultant effect on ecology.

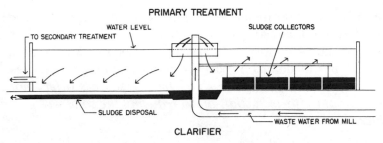

Figure 9-17. Primary treatment clarifier diagram. (*Courtesy International Paper Co.*)

Major Items Recycled

For economic reasons, recycling percentages are as follows for several major items:

Aluminum 48%
Copper   61%
Steel   26%
Paper   20%

There is an almost endless list of other items, such as automobile tires, glass, and plastics, that should be recycled to a greater extent and will be when the necessary pressure is applied—either natural or legal, or both. Since we shall have to do this eventually, why don't we start to accelerate recycling now?

In the forest products industry we are fortunate that wood is an agricultural product which can be harvested and regrown. This fact is counterbalanced by the fact that it is possible to harvest faster than regrowth. While industry is constantly planting new trees on harvested land, this replanting is only one of many efforts that must be made on behalf of mankind.

"Energy" dominates civilization. No decent living standard is possible without it. Depletion of coal and oil reserves, which have taken millions of years to accumulate, must be slowed down drastically by substituting alternatives. Forest product waste can be one source of fuel.

Another important item affecting living standards is solid waste disposal. Since a large part of the population is concentrated in metropolitan or suburban areas, garbage disposal is a major concern, both in the billions of dollars of cost for removal and in burial sites. *It is elementary that recycling our recoverable resources offers monetary reward for our efforts in addition to reducing the solid waste removal problem.*

Lower Energy Requirements

When we reclaim used wood fibers, less energy is required to reduce them to their fibrous state ready for reuse than that needed to process them in the first place. One of the major problems for the manufacturer who uses recycled wood fibers as a raw material is to assure that the supply will be continuous. The process of recycling is different from that of separating virgin fiber, especially in the first stage.

Still another plus for the recycling effort and its use of less energy conversion is the fact that there is also less air, land, and water pollution. The evidence is overwhelming.

When our leaders in all forms of government get behind this effort to recycle our natural resources by passing stringent laws and offering tax incentives, we shall be back on the right track. In the meantime, as consumers, we must cooperate with our local recycling drives. Let's all enjoy a better environment.

INDEX

ABOUT THE AUTHOR

David Saltman has spent 30 of the past 35 years as a buyer of printing. Currently president of Elgin Press, New York, which he founded in 1960, Mr. Saltman began his career in 1940 in the production department of Cowan Publishing Corp., publishers of electronics trade magazines. He also spent 5 years in the United States Army, for which he volunteered in 1941 and from which he was mustered out in 1945 as a combat-seasoned captain of artillery.

After rejoining Cowan Publishing in 1946, Mr. Saltman began taking special courses to improve his skills as a magazine production manager. Working days as a printing buyer, he spent his evenings attending Columbia and New York Universities, touring printing plants, and attending sessions of the many graphic arts clubs that afford opportunity for further education in the New York area. He took so many courses and did so well in them that in 1952 New York University hired him to teach a magazine production course in its evening School of General Studies. He has been teaching the course ever since, and is currently an adjunct assistant professor. He also teaches at the evening school of the Printing Industries of Metropolitan New York.

Since the 1940s, Mr. Saltman has bought, planned, and sold millions of dollars worth of printing of all types and for many purposes. He has toured hundreds of printing facilities in the metropolitan New York area including those of customers and printers whom he serves as a consultant. Through his contacts in those pursuits and in lecturing and graphic arts club activities, he has kept himself fully informed on the many developments that are making printing one of the most rapidly changing technologies in the world.

Writing about those changes in the graphic arts press has helped to earn Mr. Saltman several Golden Key awards from the International Club of Printing House Craftsmen, a citation from the National Association of Recycling Industries, and listings in *Who's Who in the East*, *Who's Who in the United States*, and the *Dictionary of International Biography*. His column, "Print Plan Problem Solving," is a regular feature of *Printing Impressions*.

The author has served as president of the Productioneers and the Navigators and has held committee chairmanship with such groups as the American Institute of Graphic Arts and the Association of Publication Managers.

Mr. Saltman has lectured before the Business Paper Editors Association, the National Business Press, the House Magazine Institute, the Purchasing Managers Association, and the American Management Association (serving AMA as a seminar chairman as well as a guest lecturer). He also chaired two seminars at the Printing Industry Association of the South.

Mr. Saltman is a member of the Association of Graphic Arts Consultants of Printing Industries of America. He is the author of *Production Planning & Impositions Simplified*, published by the North American Publishing Corp.

In World War II, his combat service, with the 6th Tank Destroyer Group, 10th Armored Division, X111 Corps, saw him through the Normandy, Ardennes, and Central Europe Campaigns. Lieutenant Colonel Saltman graduated from the Army Command and General Staff College in 1961. He was a C & GS instructor for several years in the Army Reserve School.

PAPER BASICS
By David Saltman

Paper is indispensable. Yet, although it is one of America's major industries, even the rudiments of paper manufacture are still mysterious to most of us. Here is a readable, practical approach to understanding paper—where it comes from, how it is made, and how best to use it for maximum efficiency. An excellent introduction for professionals in several fields as well as for general readers, the book is thoroughly up-to-date, covering the newest technological advances and exploring the urgent challenges of environmental and energy conservation in paper production.

The author describes how the forest products industry harvests and regrows trees, and explains how good forest management is used for the highest possible yield of wood per acre. The pulp and paper manufacturing process is concisely explained—transportation, chipping, and debarking of the trees; groundwood and chemical pulping; bleaching and refining; and forming, sizing, coating, calendering, and sheeting. The main equipment used (such as continous digesters, fourdriniers, and twin wire formers) is described and clearly illustrated. Presenting the characteristics of different types of paper—newsprint, offset, bond, text, bristol, index, and tag—the author shows how to use each one to best advantage, discussing such variables as rag content and coating.

For purchasing agents in publishing and advertising, how to buy paper is examined in depth. Chapters on the terminology and mathematics of paper purchase define basis weight and clarify the industry's notoriously confusing price structure. Many useful charts and tables provide such information as comparative weights and bulks, postage factors, and metric conversions. Handy formulas are included for such important procedures as determining weights and calculating signatures and multiples. Sound suggestions on how to

(Continued on back flap)